AMBITION

WIN AT LIVING

MICHAEL FULMORE

Library of Congress Control Number: 2013900739
ISBN: Hardcover   978-1-4797-7878-2
                     Softcover   978-1-4797-7877-5
                     Ebook   978-1-4797-7879-9

To order additional copies of this book, contact:
Xlibris Corporation
1-888-795-4274
www.Xlibris.com
Orders@Xlibris.com
124419

TABLE OF CONTENTS

PART ONE: LIVE AND NOT TOLERATE

PART TWO: EVERYTHING IS NOT WORTH IT

PART THREE: MAKE PEOPLE BELIEVE YOU

PART FOUR: WALK AWAY

PART FIVE: BECAUSE YOU CAN

PART ONE:
LIVE AND NOT TOLERATE

CHAPTER 1:
LIVE AND NOT TOLERATE

LIFE IS MEANT TO BE lived and not tolerated. We go through life tolerating ups and downs. We tolerate what people say to us, and we tolerate things that we feel like we just can never change, rather, this is not the essence of life nor is it the reason why we are alive. We were not born in this world just to tolerate whatever comes our way. Having high goals, we are meant to live out our lives to the fullest.

To live means to change things. To live, one needs to affect other people. To live means to make a purposeful, conscious act to get something done in this earth. To tolerate is to easily lie on your back and cry about your situation, thinking that the world is against you. Just sitting back and never doing anything

> *We were not born in this world just to tolerate whatever comes our way.*

productive or constructive only creates misery. But to live life is to take your mind and your body and all your bones and put them all together to make something great—something worth looking at, something worth admiring, and something worth the time of other people. You are a living being. A living being is to live passionately. A living being is not just to be observant, wanting to see and hear what others are doing. We learn many things. We read many books. We hear many speakers, preachers, and people talk, still we rarely take the initiative to live complete lives. We cannot be people of only theory and no practice. It makes a difference when you make a conscious decision to live out what you know and believe. There is much on the inside of you that has probably lain dormant for some time. Tolerating failure and mediocrity should have always been beneath you. What purpose does it serve to keep your inner ability bottled up if it could change the lives of many? Be great and don't accept mediocrity or, better yet, don't tolerate mediocrity. Be excellent and don't tolerate anything less. Be who you're supposed to be, and don't tolerate accepting the identity of somebody else or the identity that someone gave you. You'll always have to tell yourself to come out of toleration and into living life. Consciously living your life is extremely important. Ask yourself, "What have I tolerated in my life?" Is it negative thoughts, negative people, negative attitudes, or a destructive lifestyle? What is it that is keeping you from achieving being who you

> *The moment your level of tolerance changes for any specific thing, that thing must change.*

know you are supposed to be? There are many dangers in possessing a high tolerance for mediocrity. Having the wrong tolerance can and will hold you back. Having the wrong tolerance can make you believe that something that should be far removed from you has a right to be in your life.

Ask yourself what you have tolerated and allowed to go on in your life. When you figure this out, change it. When your level of tolerance changes, your life will change. Many times what we don't want will stay around us because we allow it to be there. For instance, if you want a good night's sleep, then you can't allow calamity in your bedroom. If you desire to increase in creativity, then you can't spend a lot of time around uncreative people. The moment your level of tolerance changes for any specific thing, that thing must change.

BOUNCE BACK

Progress. It doesn't come without setbacks and the opportunity to bounce back quickly. Don't take too many years, too many months, too many weeks, and too many days to bounce back from one experience. Too often following a single incident, people spend the remainder of their lives thinking about it or living out the hurt of one experience with one individual. As a person of progress and as a person of growth, you must learn to bounce back quickly. A bad moment was only supposed to last for that moment. Don't let a bad experience that lasted for three minutes turn into three years, or even worse, thirty years of negative outlooks. If someone broke your heart or burned you on a deal, then leave it in the past and don't expect every person that you encounter to do the same. You have to live for today and think about the future. Keep your future goals in your mind and in your thoughts, and meditate on them daily. When a bad situation happens (and they will because that's life), you'll be able to recover quickly because your focus is on something else. I've met many, many people that can't do what needs to be done right now because of what was done to them in their past. It is sad when a twenty-year-old can't perform as a twenty-year-old should even though he or she has the body, mind, and the skill to do so because of what happened to them when he or she was fifteen. I've seen many people, even elderly people, who stay stuck on what happened to them when they first began their adult lives. They fell in love and someone broke their heart. They were interested in a business and lost a lot of money, or they were just so zealous about life and then life came crashing down on them. And now at sixty years old, they have had the same job for thirty years. They are married to someone they don't like because they don't like themselves, and they just go on in life, absorbing the motions and never exceeding or excelling to anything better. What a shame to have so much and have so little at the same time. If you don't bounce back, then you allow your circumstances and situations to bounce all over you. That is not life; that is a slow death. You were created to do great things, to explore different things in life, to change the status quo, and simply to be you. So you must give diligence, perseverance, and an absolutely unbreakable will toward accomplishing what's in your heart. Even as you experience bumps in the road don't take pleasure in a pity party; you may grieve for a moment, but let the moment just be a moment. Don't make your moments longer than they have to be. There is a secret art in bouncing back. The best people, the greatest achievers, and the most productive people don't necessarily have the best scheduling system, they simply learned how to recover from setbacks quickly.

> *A bad moment was only supposed to last for that moment.*

They can be flexible and therefore continue to move forward even though things change, as they always do. I've learned to use every mistake and setback to my advantage. It's similar to an artist who spots a mistake on her artwork. When she makes an error, she can attempt to completely remove it (which may damage the entire canvas) or use it to her advantage. The error could become something that was never created or thought of before. Think of the things that you go through as indicators of different routes you may need to take, different actions you may need to take, and different people you may need to team up with. Bad things are not all that bad when you can use them to your advantage.

Don't Give Up Too Soon

There is never a good reason to give up; however, I've had good reasons to simply move on. Don't ever mistake one for the other. Giving up is simply quitting because your situation outlasts your endurance. Moving on is when you know you can do something better and you decide to no longer stick to something that is beneath you. Now let's talk more about giving up. Why do people give up? Why should you not give up? Why is it really a bad thing to give up on something you really believe in? It doesn't matter who agrees with you or who doesn't agree with you about your goals. Your visions will always be clearer to you than they are to other people. Don't be frustrated if what's achievable to you is not conceivable to others. With that level of clarity, go forward, and keep going forward until you accomplish what you saw in your mind, what you felt in your heart, and what you pictured in your dreams. If you decide to give up, then what was the point of starting? If you ever feel like giving up on your dreams, let that feeling be a greater reason why you shouldn't. Imagine yourself finally accomplishing what you set out to do, your own personal self-worth increasing, and having a great testimony to go along with your success. It's not admirable when someone gives up at their darkest moment, even though it's understandable. The testimony that inspires people says, "When I should have given up, I didn't give up, and here are the results". To be a light to people, you want to be something that

> *Giving up is simply quitting because your situation outlasts your endurance.*

people aspire to be. No one admires a quitter, or better yet, what I like to call a loser. Nothing makes the success as great as the possibility of defeat or the possibility of failure. Nothing is more satisfying to the soul than to achieve what you set out to achieve; nonetheless, you must see your decision through to the end to get the result you want. The result you want will never happen if you give up too soon. I've heard people say they gave up on a dream after two years, or after three years, even after ten years, throughout those years they did the same things, talked to the same people, and never made any necessary changes. When you decide never to give up, change will always be necessary. Deciding not to give up not only means committing yourself to your goals, but also committing yourself to being innovative as well. Be a person of change. Be a person who's not afraid of possibilities. Doing the same failing things over and over can tempt anyone to give up. Simply changing how you pursue your goals will cause a major shift in your professional and business life.

LIVING

Living is breathing your own breath and not sucking up someone else's. Living is a little bit of autonomy, mastery, and purpose mixed into one person. It is a joy to lead yourself without the interruption of everybody saying what you should and shouldn't do. Becoming a master of yourself and rising above your own limitations begets a snowball effect to succeed in your life. When you discover your purpose in life, being driven from within becomes no problem. It becomes second nature, and your days are filled with only desiring to move forward.

> *Living is breathing your own breath and not sucking up someone else's.*

To be completely living is to be the total opposite of being dead. Death is inevitable; however, it should not come early in your life.

A dead man doesn't walk, breathe, think, or take action. This is what you should be completely contrary to in order to live to your greatest potential. Being contrary to death is a good thing. The idea of living successfully is contagious to the rest of your body. When your body receives signals from your brain that says to live and not to die, you begin to live in a whole new motion. Living well is thinking well.

Living is doing something that's bigger than you and bigger than what you could ever be. Life is enjoyable, so just enjoy. Life is fun, so have some of it. Life is interesting, so it is a waste of time to be one-dimensional. Life is new every day, so don't be boring. Life gives, so you should give too.

It is easy to believe that living life is only enjoyable when you're doing things that destroy your life, such as partying, smoking, drinking, etc.; however, living life to its fullest is when you are doing something that empowers not only you but also other people. We all have something

> *Living is doing something that's bigger than you and bigger than what you could ever be.*

of importance to give—something that is unique. Simply, what we all have to give is ourselves. What do I mean when I say "giving of yourself"? Well, we all have qualities that are special. Whether it's the way you see, taste, smell, touch, or observe. Whatever it is, you have a lot of it to give, and you must give a lot of it because the world can only get it from you. Be selfless enough to make sure that you do not die before the world experiences what you have to give. To accomplish this is truly living.

LIVE FOR MUCH

I have to be very honest when I say that living only for yourself is extremely boring. You will never be satisfied with yourself. If you lose weight, you want to lose more. If you're short, you want to be tall. If you're tall, you wish you were a little shorter. If your skin is light, you may want to be darker. If your skin is dark, you may want to be lighter. The list goes on and on. Change your view from just what you can gain, to what you can help others achieve. Visualize someone else becoming healthier because of you and so many more people becoming greater because of you. Release somebody else's dream. Focus on building someone else. When you can meet the needs of others, you'll discover your product, service, brand, ministry, talent, and purpose; you'll finally be fulfilled. It doesn't start with what you want; it is finding out what other people need. People who live for themselves eventually become robbers, manipulators, scam artists, or just your average crooks. Those who live so that others can benefit are the best people you will ever meet.

You'll begin to love life when you finally begin to realize all that you have to offer and all the opportunities that are out there for you to make a significant difference. Any fool can imagine themselves with a big house, cars, and nice clothes, or having some nice things for himself and his family. It takes true strength to consider what will make someone's life bigger and better. Picture yourself in front of thousands of people as they admire your services, your products, your wisdom and understanding. Your insight and all that you have developed yourself to be, reflected in what you do. Imagine their facial expressions changing from frowns and becoming smiles. Imagine a shift in their attitudes towards life. Imagine the effects you can have on people. You can literally change the lives of many if you allow changing lives to become a priority.

Believe it or not, getting the house of your dreams, possessing many cars, having lots of money in your bank account, and being totally debt-free is not as hard as people make it out to be. After you acquire all you want, which will only take a couple of years, what else do you live for? More houses for you? More cars for you? To really achieve your optimal success you must immediately put your best efforts into creating wealth and value in other people's lives. This is not to say you must live entirely for people but you must act as the conduit between people and good things.

DESERVING MORE

You deserve whatever you put yourself in a position to deserve. We are all afforded grace to some level; however, there are some things you're just going to have to do yourself. If you think you are deserving of being wealthy, put yourself in a position to receive wealth; it's really that simple. If you think you deserve a wonderful spouse, then put yourself in a position where a wonderful person would be interested in you. If you think you are deserving of good friends, good family members, and healthy children, put yourself in a position to receive those things. Don't just be a pie-in-the-sky dreamer. Be a right-now doer. If you are positioned well, then who can stop you? And if they're in your way, being in the right position will move them out of your

> *If you are positioned well, then who can stop you?*

way. Think about people who we consider important. They command the time of other people. An important person is considered important not just because of their gender, race, or education, but because they have done something that is of significance. So if I do something of significance, have I earned the right to be called important? YES! And with my importance, I can be deserving of people's time. I don't deserve anyone's money unless I serve them a product and/or service so beneficial to their lives that they begin to throw their money at me. Possessing successful concepts in life are not that difficult; they just require you to do them. When successful concepts become a part of your life, you will never go back to old failing ways, failing thoughts, and failing speech patterns. Once you realize your own potential, you'll never want to go back to mediocrity.

HAVE LOW TOLERANCE FOR THE RIGHT THINGS

For a while, I couldn't figure out why people would stay in certain situations or with certain people. Then I had an "aha" moment. Tolerance! People who have a high tolerance for something will tolerate it no matter how good or bad it is. The strange thing is that most people have a high tolerance for the wrong thing, and a low tolerance for good things. Isn't that strange? People will have a high tolerance for stress, anxiety, and worry. On the other end, people will have a low tolerance for happiness, joyfulness, and good relationships. They would rather just believe it's too good to be true. Having a high tolerance for destructive things… this is surely a recipe for failure. I've witnessed people tolerate physical abuse from someone who was actually weaker than they were. Psychologically, they just accepted being abused, for whatever strange reason. I've seen people tolerate their own loneliness as if they were not good enough to be around other good people. It takes a lot of convincing yourself to tolerate something that you know is killing you, strangling you, and making you a worse person. Nothing that causes you only to look forward to death should ever be allowed in your life. Using your same intelligence, strength, mind, heart, and spirit, to convince yourself that you are good enough and that there are certain things you would no longer accept or tolerate in your life. Life is too good to end your life because of one bad event, or one failed relationship, or one bad circumstance.

Do not let years pass by before you finally say, "No!" No to failing jobs, no to horrible relationships, no to addictions, and no to fears. Just say no. Choose what you will and will not tolerate; once you make those decisions, then there's a lot of things you will never deal with again—not because they don't show up, but because you won't tolerate it. Have a high tolerance for joy, laughter, positivity, peace, and good people. Accept good in your life no matter what direction it came from; good is good. You don't have to accept everything that comes your way; be patient enough to wait for good things to come. And they will come as long as you position yourself and have a

> *Life is too good*
> *to end your life*
> *because of one bad*
> *event, or one failed*
> *relationship, or one*
> *bad circumstance.*

higher tolerance for them. Being empathetic and compassionate doesn't mean tolerating negative attitudes, negative views, or pessimistic ideas. Before you read another self-help book or positive-thinking book, your tolerance level can change right now, which will force other things in your life to change immediately. Give diligence to the important things in your life and don't tolerate the unimportant things.

NEVER TOLERATE AGAIN

Don't lie to yourself. Admit it. You know the things that make you unproductive. Everything that you tell yourself is alright, that's really not alright, will eventually lead you to self-destruct. If you see your destruction ahead and it has not come yet, then you definitely have a chance to make some significant changes. You will always have to guard yourself from going in the direction of failure. We oftentimes are forced to take care of the right now, though the right-now responsibilities may not always lead you to where you want to be. It is imperative that you never become too involved with things that could send you on a path contrary to where you want to be.

First, allow yourself to accept change; change is good. Comfortableness has been and will always be success's worst enemy. Give yourself the chance to finally surpass even your own expectations by simply being honest with yourself. Ask yourself the question, "Do I have the right friends?" Or do you have people around you just because you have known them for years. Do I have the right habits? What do I allow myself to be distracted with? Do I reach for my goals, or do I tell myself that maybe someday I'll get there? As real as you have made your excuses, you can make your dreams a reality as well. Seriously consider what needs to be put in your life and what needs to be taken out. Doing this alone will alter your life in a profound way. Remember, there will never be a perfect time to get things right; just do it now.

> *You will always have to guard yourself from going in the direction of failure.*

WHAT AM I TOLERATING?

We tolerate a lot nowadays. E-mail overload, texting overload, Facebook messages overload—the list goes on. Even though most people would say that they can't live without the millions of distractions they get every day, the truth is just the opposite. If a normal person would take a break from TV, cell phones, and tablets for a week, he would realize that he only needed to make a few calls and a few texts and that he doesn't need to check Facebook every five minutes, giving him extra hours of productivity every week. Most people say they don't have the time to do the important things they are advised to do. Truthfully, they simply tolerate not having the time. If they would eliminate foolish activities from their lives, then they would open their doors up to some more important things.

When you tolerate good things, they grow like flowers; when you tolerate bad things, they grow too, like fungus. This is simply making an attitude change. Attitude has always been more important than your challenges.

> *Be satisfied with nothing and always strive to achieve more.*

Don't be like the average person that never lives up to her potential; don't be the next wishful thinker. Your best days are always ahead; your greatest moments and greatest relationships are still to come. If you stop now, then you will never realize entirely and holistically who you are. Be satisfied with nothing and always strive to achieve more. There's no such thing as standing still, there's only going backward or forward. If you realize right now that you are far more than what you've allowed yourself to be valued as, then you will realize there's a lot more life that you are entitled to. As long as you position yourself and put yourself in the right places, then there are no limits. There are no limits to what you can do; you can do much more than you ever dreamed possible.

STOP TOLERATING THINGS

Coming to grips with your purpose is always the first step toward achieving great things in business, finance, ministry, or anything. As long as you don't know who you are, morally anything can go, and it becomes quite difficult to take a stand for anything. Your tolerance level changes when your sense of identity, sense of self, and sense of purpose become illuminated and enlightened. Most people will try to accomplish the outer works without developing and achieving the inner works first. For instance, a liar can never do well with others because a liar can't do well with himself. A manipulator could never help people the way they need to be helped. The problem is not what you want to achieve, it is are you the right person to actually do it? Not to say that you'll never become that person, you'll need to develop key characteristics that will lead you into a successful life, and that's not just having a lot of money. When your identity and sense of self are strong, then there are many things you will no longer tolerate. And then there are many things that you will allow in your life that you rejected for so long.

Give your energy to the things that matter the most.

I had investment ideas that were rejected for so long based on the advice of other people. As I developed my own understanding, I was then able to make my own decisions pertaining to investing. This may be different for you. What is it about you that you that you are not aware of? Has someone told you to stay away from something that you always wanted to do and now you are afraid to do it? It may be time to reject what you have accepted and accept what you have rejected.

Think of this for a second: if your tolerance level changes toward and against certain things, you will literally open up doors in your life that have been there forever. A person who knows who they are won't permit certain things. This is not to say you shouldn't be open-minded, compassionate, and empathetic; this is to say that there are some things you cannot give attention or energy to. Give your energy to the things that matter the most and allow yourself to have a high tolerance for the ups and downs that come with achieving your goals. As for the naysayers, brownnosers, backbiters, and gunslingers, you should have a zero tolerance for their attitudes and negative ways, thinking, speech patterns, and thoughts. Give your life a chance to succeed by not tolerating what your life doesn't have to embrace. Let confusion and calamity be something that happen outside of you and not inside of you. The world can go crazy during every recession, not you, you're different. Be so entangled with your destiny that your current issues don't even exist. Be so driven from within that your inner force pushes things out of your way for you. It is amazing what you can do with a sense of purpose and zero tolerance for nonsense. Your new life is waiting for you; don't tolerate the unnecessary.

BELIEVING AGAIN

Death is an inevitable thing but not always a necessary thing. Many times, people allow the death of a dream or purpose or destiny to happen. Your goals in life should never die before you do, so allow yourself to dream again and believe again, and because of that, your heart will be on a different beat; your mind will think at a new rate, and your soul will have a new leap. Consider the fact that there are senior citizens who will go back to school to get their degrees, on the contrary there are twenty-year-olds who won't even get out of bed. What is the difference—a belief, a hope, or an idea that they can be better than what they are right now. So age doesn't mean a thing; ethnicity doesn't mean a thing. The reasons that we give ourselves for failure are always ridiculous. There is no reason for you to fail. There has never been a good reason to fail nor will there ever be. There will always be billions of reasons why you should display to this world your talents and abilities. Believe again that you are valuable; believe that you can do anything just like when you were a child and all things were possible. Life tends to steal people's faith and beliefs; however, it's up to you to maintain and protect them. Dream big, think big, and do big; if you're going to do anything good, you should do it in a big way. Believe in yourself. I know a lot of people say believing in yourself is prideful. If you don't believe in yourself, then how will other people believe in

> *Believe again that you are valuable.*

you? Believe in your values. Believe in your abilities. Believe that you are competent and intelligent enough to achieve what you set out to do. Don't wait for someone to believe for you.

It can be a challenge to maintain great enthusiasm. Challenges will come, and days will come that will directly impact your hope and enthusiasm. In a moment, you could be riding high and something can happen to bring you down. When this happens, see your opposition as fuel to your internal fire. To put fuel in a car, it cannot be moving. If something stops you, it is only so that you can fuel up. Some of us have had more fuel breaks than others. If that be the case, then your passion should be greater than others. Every obstacle is a chance for you to succeed again and again and again and again. There is pleasure, great pleasure, in conquering yourself and your challenges. The proof of who you are is in how you respond to your obstacles. Never again should you fear the opportunity to prove why you believe so much in your dreams.

CHAPTER 2:
YOU ARE IMPORTANT

EVERYTHING ABOUT YOU CHANGES WHEN you see yourself differently. It is easy to believe that someone who has already gained success can be successful. It's even easier to imagine yourself in their position or doing the same things that they're doing. It's a little more difficult to see yourself doing what you want to do when you're trying to live out someone else's dream. Begin to see yourself in a greater position. It may be difficult but intentionally see yourself better, smarter, and more achieved. You should have great faith in all the good things you will become. Take a leap of faith toward pursuing a journey of excellence—living better, thinking better, talking better, collaborating and connecting with different people. Not to say that there are such things as bad people; still, there are such things as different calibers of people. There are some people who want more, and there are some people who don't; as for me, I want more, so I prefer being around people that want more and seek to achieve more in life. People that seek to provide for other people and seek to do contribute to society will always inspire the best in you. No matter how much they achieve, they always stay hungry. I love people that stay hungry—not

> *Everything about you changes when you see yourself differently.*

greedy, but hungry. There's a difference: greedy people seek to steal, kill, and destroy; greedy people seek to destroy all and cause disruption. The hungry and young at heart give themselves for the benefit of society and generations to come. Remember, your own ability increases or decreases based on the company you keep. Keep a life pointed in the right direction by keeping the right people around you.

THIS IS WHY YOU'RE IMPORTANT

You are important because you have something to offer. People will see you as important because of what you can do and provide for others that is beneficial. The more you can provide, the more important you become. It is simply finding out the important qualities you have and capitalizing on them. The industry, business, or market you have a great passion about is probably where you will give and produce the most. Therefore, that's where "you're important" will come alive. That is where you will find out who and what groups need your ideas and enthusiasm. That is where you'll discover who needs your time, your services, your understanding, and your expertise. The people that will deem you as important and will give you the boost you need are discovered by simply defining what great service you can give to the masses. "You're important" exceeds far beyond the people in your family or your circle of friends. There are probably millions of people that would deem you as important if you successfully convey to them what benefit you bring to their lives. Your ability to care, create, understand, or even your experience can all serve as a means to improve other people's lives. Use what you have in a great way, and you'll render a great service to the world which will create a demand for you.

Be very intentional in your development, education, marketing, promoting, and innovation so that your importance is not lost but gained and multiplied. At the end of the day, people will want to do business with you. It is not necessarily your business or corporation people do business with, it is you. So it is important that people understand why your importance has great significance to others' improvement and growth. Become so important that others feel important around you. Become so important that you draw and pull at the importance of other people. Believe that you can make other people better. Don't ever lose your importance because we, the world, need you. General value is determined by what an asset can produce, and as you produce more, you become a greater asset. You can literally determine your own worth in the marketplace. The closest you can get to true financial freedom is by becoming so important that those who have the money in any given market seek you out for what you provide. Don't be afraid to display your worth, for you can render no greater service to the general public than to give them a solution to their problems. So where does your "you're important" matter? Well, I guess you have to find out. Go for it.

WHAT MAKES SOMEONE IMPORTANT

The characteristics and qualities of a person that is considered important are not that many. Don't get me wrong, we're not talking about your spiritual or personal worth but your worth in the marketplace. God sees you as extremely valuable no matter what. Fulfilling a need for millions can turn an unknown individual to a well-sought-out pioneer.

The key is before you. To produce anything outwardly, you much start the production internally. You can't give what you don't have. Your good business, service, career, or relationship will always begin with the personal philosophy you retain. If you have a self-sabotaging personal philosophy, then you immediately kill your chances of developing any kind of life of significance. Always be willing to change or redefine you own personal philosophy for the sake of creating the life you want. Whatever you want you can have just so long as you are willing to possess the right personal philosophy to have it. Don't define your personal philosophy by what the majority of people agree with. Public opinion will only get you the results of the majority of the public. To really reach your peak significance, you must be fueled by something other than other people's claps. Compliments don't make you important—neither do hype or accolades. Kudos wear out, hype fades away, and accolades can easily be forgotten. Importance is defined by fulfilling a need consistently, which can only be done by possessing the right philosophy. For instance, if a person believes that wealth is reserved for a select few, then they would have counted themselves out of potentially achieving great wealth. Clearly, a person cannot achieve the opposite of their own beliefs and personal philosophy. The moment your own personal beliefs and philosophy change, you then release yourself to achieve what you want. Achieving more and becoming more important to society is now available to you. By first retaining the proper philosophy, you can fulfill a need in society consistently.

> *To really reach your peak significance, you must be fueled by something other than other people's claps.*

WHAT DOES MY IMPORTANCE MEAN

Your importance means that someone's life is going to improve. Your importance means that someone who wanted to give up on life will no longer desire that. Still, your importance must be first discovered and explored. This is actually the fun part of life because the more you go deeper in your exploration of your self-importance, the more you'll find out about yourself. Your importance means that you have a chance to live a fulfilling life. Don't hesitate for one moment on your purpose; believe that you have something to give and offer to the world. It is absolutely selfish for you to hold back your talents, gifts, and abilities. Make it your top priority to develop your importance. This world needs you.

Declare that you are important starting today.

Start your day with these declarations:

I am important.

I am worthy.

I am worth the chance and risk.

I am worth others' time.

My importance will change this world.

UNIMPORTANT THINGS DON'T MATTER

Don't give unimportant things consistent attention. The more you indulge in unimportant things, the more your value decreases. Defining something as unimportant is simple. If it doesn't help you or others, it does not deserve consistent attention and energy. Why waste days out of the week hypnotized by your TV or hours in a day in unproductive relationships? These things take your strength, time, energy, and focus. It would be wise to take all this effort into important matters. Ask yourself what serves your life in a meaningful way. Who helps you, and better yet, who do you help when you are around each other? This is not something that you probably can think of in one sitting. Take the time to answer these questions. When you find the answers, don't ignore the facts. Whatever you discover in your findings, this is what will always be true; it's time for change.

> *Your life doesn't have to be a bag full of wishes.*

We all experience a day, a week, or a month going past faster than we could keep up with, or money being spent faster than we would have liked for it to be. The same is true with your time, energy, resources, and abilities. They are spent far quicker than what you realize. If they're not carefully delegated, you run the risk of losing what you thought you always would have. Spend time thinking and planning away from the unimportant things in your life. Sometimes it is easier to figure out what not to do before you figure out what to do. After you figure out what not to do, stay away from those things. This forces your mind to consider other things—other things that are more important and enlightening. This challenges the urge we all have to settle for less. There is a great ease in not challenging yourself and in settling for what is here right now. That ease could be your worst enemy. Easiness will make you feel relaxed and complacent toward your goal. To be in this condition makes you susceptible (maybe instead of acceptable? Up to you!) to unproductive and unimportant behaviors. Be considerate enough of your future to recognize when ease has become acceptable in your life. Embracing complacency is the best way to ensure a life of hopeful wishes. Your life doesn't have to be a bag full of wishes. Your life can live up to the expectations that you have or once had for yourself. Wishing is for wishers; success is for doers.

Fight the urge to settle for less.

You Are Not Someone's Opinion

Believe it or not, not everyone will agree with your success or your initiatives to achieve success. Others' thoughts about you do not create your reality, rather, those thoughts create their reality. Your own thoughts create your own reality. If you allow the negative thoughts of other people to become your own, then it is really your own thoughts that affect your life, not theirs. People will always be opinionated creatures. It's in their nature. It is your duty to be contrary to the negative thoughts and opinions people may have about you. Public opinion is simply that—public. Your own private opinions will affect you. The decision must be made: will you embrace public opinion or your private opinion?

If you embrace your own private opinions of yourself, be sure to correct them if they are filled with negativity and toxic influence from others. Even though an opinion appears to have no power, an opinion can give life to a toxic or healthy way of thinking. If you embrace the wrong opinion, you can line yourself up for the wrong thinking patterns. Opinions are generally facts to be proven. People may have opinions about a person's future or opinions about the end result of a project. Although these are opinions, they can have a great impact in the end. When a person headed in the right direction fails to ignore negative opinions that can detour them to the wrong direction, the results can be quite predictable. A child with limitless potential can be affected by the opinions of other children, and those opinions can create a hideous adulthood. I hope this is becoming clear to you. Stand clear of negative opinions. Just as people have their right to give an opinion, you have your right to ignore their opinions.

ENCOURAGEMENT

Here is one of the most controversial things that I've learned. You should never wait for someone to encourage you, You should always take the initiative to encourage others. The most encouragement that you will ever receive is not from someone encouraging you, it will come from the fulfillment of encouraging someone else. Your enthusiasm for life increases when you take the time out to rev up someone else's enthusiasm. Be the type to make it happen for someone else. Great people bring out the greatness in others, not just in themselves. More people need your encouragement than you realize. A friend, a family member, a partner or employee, your boss, or anyone you come in contact with can use an unbiased word of encouragement from you. If you want to be at your greatest, push somebody else to their greatest. Challenge someone else to perform at their peak potential. If you're waiting for someone to encourage you, you'll probably keep on waiting. With your best voice, with your best choice of words, and with your best attitude, give encouragement to others and you'll always have encouraging words from others at the right time. A simple "Good job," "Great to see you," "Hope you're doing well," "Keep on going," or "Keep pushing" will change somebody's life. Nothing sticks to a person like the right words at the right time. New life and hope are passed on when you encourage a person's good works and efforts. Never stop being a light to someone's days. You can always be the most enthusiastic and optimistic individual in the room.

Without any hidden agendas or tricks up your sleeves, give someone an esteem boost by saying something good about them. It is always a plus for someone to associate you with something good. Words carry serious weight. A person could drop something heavy on their foot, and the result of it will not be as great as someone saying the right or wrong thing to them. A bruised foot will only last for weeks. The right or wrong words can last for a lifetime. Make meaningful and lasting impacts on people's lives. You could literally start the process of changing people's lives tomorrow. This is not a trick to make people like you, it is a chance to put into practice making impactful decisions. The moment you're consciously considering the well-being of other people is the moment your life goes into a new dimension. The best people, the best products, the best services, and the best professionals all come from first innovatively considering the benefit to other people lives.

Ask yourself this life changing question, "How can I and how will I use what I have for the growth of other people?" Asking yourself this simple question on a daily basis will cause you to consider many options that you may never have considered before. More options to choose from means the start of a new life. This new life for you can start through just encouraging others. Encouraging others will help you consistently be an outward-looking person focused on the good in others. Encouragement is just a simple thing until it is explored to its maximum use. Encouragement is not to be confused with manipulation. Manipulators are destructive and are not beneficial to others. A con man will smile to your face to only take advantage of you later. Encouragement should always be given with no strings attached. Of course, encouraging someone else can have its benefits. Of those benefits could be a new friend, partner, or open door. These benefits should not be taken advantage of. Use whatever benefits you obtain for the greater benefit of more people. This can all start by the use of your words of encouragement.

Don't Wait to Feel Important

Importance is not a feeling, even though after you realize you are of some significance to others, it'll give you a great esteem boost. We're not talking about feeling something like butterflies in your stomach when you're attracted to someone, but actually being something. Being a person of significance, value, and a necessary commodity. When you are a necessary commodity, you'll probably feel the demand for your time before any other feeling comes. You'll feel the demand to consistently produce good services and products or the demand not to go back to who you used to be. Nonetheless, these are all good, even though they may not feel so good. To do good and not feel good about it is one of the oxymorons of life. It's better to be something and not feel like it than not to be it at all. Don't focus on a feeling or a special emotion or bubble in your stomach. Nervousness can make you feel very awkward, don't take it as a sign to quit. Importance may not feel exciting all the time; nonetheless, that's not an indicator that your importance is lost. Your emotions may not always be a direct link to your success; however, your success will be very evident even if emotionally you don't agree. Never stop moving forward based on feelings. Your thoughts, your emotions, or an idea will always present itself as an opposition to your goals. The great thing is that the thoughts, emotions, and ideas are yours. As the owner of your thoughts, emotions, and ideas, you can tell them what to do. Who you are internally is not owned by another person. Begin to take authority over your internal self quickly. You can literally command yourself to do what you feel you are emotionally incapable of doing. Feelings and emotions are to help you consider things from a compassionate and empathetic perspective. Feelings and emotions are never to detour you away from making good decisions. Never put your life on hold for emotional reasons. At times, in order to debunk your emotions, you will have to be rational to move forward.

Emotions are a good thing. It's what makes humans not be robots. When emotions are out of control, they can give you false impressions and a misconstrued sense of reality. When things happen that are out of your control, that may cause a setback; don't let your emotions tell you that that's a sign to quit. In life, unexpected things will happen—which is actually one of the joys of life. The unpredictable journey of day-to-day living is not as much fun without a surprise here and there. There is nothing in life that you can't handle. So your only job is to handle it with intelligence, integrity, and character.

When you make your attempts in life, never get discouraged because you may still carry a wound from a past situation. You should look at the wound and remember how you survived. A wound is to serve as a testimony—whether the wound is physical, emotional, and/or psychological. Defeat is never represented by a wound.

LIVE A LIFE OF SIGNIFICANCE

What if you live to be eighty or older? If you think about it, that's not a lot of time. Most of the time was spent being raised, going to school, and working a job. A large majority of people won't start living their lives until later in their years. So what will you fill your day with? Will it be complaints and hopeful wishing? Or will you wake up every morning, blowing a kiss to life and being grateful for the opportunity that you have? Fill your days with the most significant of activities. This doesn't mean live a boring life; what this does mean is taking the initiative to make sure you actually live your life—exercising, reading, writing, building great relationships, or pursuing projects that are significant to others. Make your day full so that you can go to bed emptied out. A famous saying is that many people go to their grave with their song still playing in them; however, how many people go to sleep every night with things they could've done today still inside of them? You should make time for greatness every day. Realize that days quickly add up to weeks and weeks to months and months to years and years create your lifetime. Making room for greatness every day puts you in a position to live a great life and not one of regret. Living a life of significance starts with what you do in a day. When you're living in the days that you have, don't wait for the right moment—create the right moment. There are too many people waiting for somebody to discover them and waiting for the right person to show up when it has to start with what you do right now in the day that's been allotted to you. You've been allotted grace every day. Another time has been given to you for you to complete your destiny entirely. Don't spend time in front of the TV for hours a day and making the same excuses as everyone else. Only a fool believes that they're the results someone else's wrongdoing. Just as your failures are your fault, it's the same for your success; it starts with what you do. Living a life of significance begins to develop you as a significant person.

Be a problem solver, a joy bringer, and a hope giver. Let these be priorities for you. Your days are so important that you don't get them back. You can neither buy a day or exchange it over the counter. Every day is too important for it to be wasted on unimportant things. Every day you should hope for the best, achieve for the best, and do your best. You don't know it yet, but there are many people waiting for what you are to accomplish. To achieve your greatest potential on a daily basis, jam-pack your days with everything that is meaningful to your life and the lives of others. Life is not just about having free time, it's about having a great time. You owe your life the chance to improve by being selective of the things you do on a daily basis.

Self-development is to be taken into consideration on a daily basis. Without the development of self, you ruin your chances of a more fulfilling life. Self-development consists of studying, reading, and reevaluating your personal philosophy to ensure that you're not adapting to failure patterns. It is easy to ignore self-development because of the fear of what you may find out about yourself. Of course, you're going to find things about yourself you may not like, that's the beauty of self-development. You develop away from what you used to be into what you want to be.

> *You should make time for greatness every day.*

Every day, focus on organizing your life to where you want it to be and not organizing it to stay the way it is. When you're organizing your life, consider more than just the responsibilities and obligations you have right now. You must organize your life to reflect where you want to go in order to progress. Just as addictions take repetition before they become addictions, the same is true for your new life. Every day, work on taking away what you don't need in your life and adding what you do need. Eventually, depending on how bad you want your life to change, your life will finally be the life you are proud of and not the life you regret. This is not something just to hope for or just to dream of for the next two years, it is for you to take immediate action toward changing your life.

Never adapt to comfortableness. If you're not where you want to be, you probably have to change associations, habits, and speech patterns. None of this is possible in a state of comfortableness. You can be anything you want to be as long as you take the right approach toward it. Lying down and waiting does not bring about change and, therefore, is the wrong approach. Pulling and pushing every part of your being toward your goals is always the right approach. An even better approach is establishing in your heart and mind that you will not give up.

> *Eventually, depending on how bad you want your life to change, your life will finally be the life you are proud of and not the life you regret.*

WHAT DO YOU MEAN TO YOU

Confidence is a sure way to boost your energy without any kind of energy drink or shake. What is important is that your confidence is not 100 percent the result of what other people have to say about you. You're going to have to believe in yourself before anybody else does. You must realize your dream before anybody else realizes it for you. People can make you feel good with their words, with their actions, or with their gifts; however, you must be driven from within to maintain authentic confidence. It is your own thoughts that will keep you going or slow you down, or even worse, stop you.

So what do you mean to you? You're probably very clear on what others mean to you or what you mean to others. A question that a person should always ask themselves is what they mean to themselves. Do they mean a little to themselves or do they mean a lot? Some may believe asking this question is the beginning of being conceited. Only a fool would think that humility is thinking horribly of yourself. How you see yourself is how you force others to see you. How you see yourself determines what you allow yourself to do and not do. How you see yourself will keep you where you are or free you to different places in life. So I ask you again, what do you mean to you? Well, only you know. Don't run from this question. Answer it. When you answer it, be honest. If the answer's not good, address the issue. You should see yourself as creative, beautiful, smart, intelligent, able, willing, and teachable.

Begin to see yourself in a new way. For some, this may be more difficult—not because you are less of a person than someone else, it could be because of past experiences that may hinder you from enjoying yourself in a positive way. I remember a song that says, "free your mind and the rest will follow." This is such a true statement. Everything that I've ever done in my life that was new for me at the time was always the result of me first believing I can do it in my mind. You are not dumb, unintelligent, unworthy, or less than anybody else. As a matter of fact, once you realize who you are and what you mean to yourself, you will see that others actually need you. Possess the best thoughts for yourself. Never give up on yourself even if the world does.

The world may never actually give up on you, even if you've personally experienced many people in your world giving up on you. It is then that you learn to lace up your own boot straps and believe even harder in what you know is still possible. Time is a friend to those who do not quit and for those who do not back down. Time is the enemy to those who do not have the patience or the wherewithal to see things through. So again I ask, what do you mean to you? Are you important enough to yourself? Because if you are important to yourself, then you believe that you are worth good health, intelligent decisions, good friendships, and a better life. No matter how tough things are or the obstacles that are ahead, you have yet to see your greatest achievements. Keep going.

YOUR THOUGHTS MATTER

What you see and how you see something can bring a new perspective that has been missing. New industries, new products, and new services blossom from the seed of a new idea. Never stop fueling your creative engine. Never stop believing and innovating. Without creativity and innovation, we are headed toward extinction. Your thoughts, ideas, inventions, and innovative changes can be just what society needs. Learn to explore your thoughts and eventually bring them to the market. Test the originality of your ideas. Go to sleep with your ideas on your mind, and by the time you wake up, you'll probably have additional thoughts to go with your initial idea. The fruits of your thoughts are worthy of being developed.

Always effectively research your ideas. Having good thoughts and supreme creativity is not enough. Life must be brought to your ideas. Be brave enough to believe in your ideas first before anybody else calls them good or gives them a thumbs-up. Make your ideas great and worthy of attention. If you know you have a good idea, then the world simply has to catch up to you. When presenting your ideas to others, creatively package them so that anybody can experience the same enlightenment that you did when you first had that thought. If someone doesn't agree with your ideas, then they just don't get it yet. Some ideas are so great that before their time, others just cannot grasp them. If you grasp your idea, don't lower your standards because others don't quite grasp them yet.

Your thoughts and ideas have probably been disregarded at some point. And I say to that, who cares? Who cares if you had a bad idea before? You'll probably have another one. Who cares if your ideas didn't work the first time? It happens; what matters is that you never stop pushing out the greatness that lives in you. Basketball players eventually will hit a bad shot. A soccer player will eventually make a bad kick. You will probably do a few things in your life that might not work out so well. And to that I say, life doesn't get any better. Mess-ups, miscalculations, and bad choices will benefit you as long as you use them to create something better and more beautiful. Shutting down your creative engine is not an option. You are just a few steps from your greatest thoughts and breakthroughs. Your chances at success increase the more you diligently focus your thoughts and intelligence on the right things.

Your mind is always considering, calculating, and developing new thoughts. By filling your mind with the right stuff, you give your thoughts great ammunition. With this ammunition, you'll be shooting out world-changing ideas. Don't ever hold back your creative flow again. People need the amazing ideas that are hidden in your mind. Your experiences and your past interactions have all helped to create the person you are today. You possess what can significantly help others.

CHAPTER 3:
ANOTHER CHANCE IS GIVEN EVERY DAY

PEOPLE WHO ARE FAILURES, FOR the most part, choose to be failures. One mistake—one mess up—and that's it; they give up for the rest of their lives, here is what I've learned: if you're going to be successful, you're actually going to fail a lot. Failing a lot is not a problem, it's what you do with the failure that matters. Will you learn the lessons that are given from your failures or will you fold your arms and give up? Will you make a life-changing decision and say, "I will not give up, and I will continue pursuing what I first set out to achieve"? One bad day cannot dictate your entire life; one bad day simply teaches you what not to repeat the next day. You have twenty-four hours in a day; the best thing you can do to start a good day off is to make as much time in the day available as it is possible for you to achieve what you set out to achieve; in other words, don't sleep all day. Don't drink all day. Don't smoke all day or spend all your days chasing skirts; you only have twenty-four hours in a day. If you progress in doing unproductive activities for the most part of your day and continue for many, many days, you will live an unproductive life. If you spend your twenty-four hours filling them with productive activities, lo and behold, you'll have a productive life. Take some time to evaluate your days and what you do in those days. If you can effectively figure out which part of your days are the most unproductive and change those moments into productive moments, you will begin the process of literally changing your life.

Begin to change your perspective of what a day means to you. A day is not an opportunity to just go back to work. A day is not an opportunity to just hear your nagging children or nagging spouse. A day is given to you—literally given to you—as a gift for you to use wisely, shrewdly, effectively, and intelligently, your God-given abilities so you can make the best of each moment of that day. Don't try to live out your entire week in a day, live in each day and see what you can do to make the most out of each day. I'm excited when I think about what the day may bring because I have repositioned myself for the day to bring me the best for that day. That could be good news, a new friend, or anything that can bring value to my life. It took some time to get my days to be the way that they are. You can literally reconstruct your days; you can add to or take away from whatsoever you choose of your days. Whatever goes on in those twenty-four hours, seven days in a week, and 365 days in a year, you can reconstruct by adding or taking out certain people, activities, places, or things. You can literally make your day what you want it to be.

You Do Have a Chance

Sometimes your chances at something can completely run out. Many people are not even close to their chances running out on accomplishing their dreams and life purposes. The idea of who they really can be still resonates in their minds. So to answer the question on how many chances you get, well, multiple chances are given every day. Or better yet, a chance is given once you give yourself a chance. Give yourself a chance to do what you should've done years ago. Give yourself a chance to accomplish what other people told you couldn't be done. A closed door in your life can come by closing your mind first. If your mind is closed to everything, then nothing is available to you—not even another chance. If you loosen the tightly screwed bolts that you put on your mind, then you will turn the knob on the doors in your life. Chance after chance will seem to show up miraculously. Keeping your mind open one hundred times will give you one hundred chances. A shut door, an undiscovered opportunity, or the clarity for your next move in life is just waiting for you to open your mind.

Don't Wait Until the Day Is Over

To sit or lie around all day, waiting for the day to be over, is a recipe for failure. Waiting for success will never get you to it. Hoping that it will come without the proper action won't get you there, either. I watched many friends and families profess the same words: "I can't wait till the day is over." Many times, my friends and families will be referring to their job or school; no matter what they are referring to, this is a horrible mentality to have. It is this mentality that people carry around for years—angry at the life that they chose or angry at the career path that they chose or schooling that they picked. What a waste to know that something is not for you; and you stay in it out of comfort. A day should be filled with learning and growth and positive interaction. Just waiting for the day to be over leaves you powerless. You only wait for things that are out of your power. The things you do in your day are absolutely within your own power. Do something about everything that is within your power in that day if you're not satisfied with it. No more waiting. It is now time to take action. Even though there are some things you have to wait on, don't turn everything into a waiting game. In most cases, the day that a person is experiencing now is the result of decisions made over many years of time. A day that is filled with an eight-hour job and multiple responsibilities, appointments, and obligations doesn't just happen overnight. Your life is the direct result of what you made of it. I know this is a harsh reality. This is the reality that we all must face in order to change it. If you can take that you made your life into what it is, then you can begin to move forward.

There are some things that are out of your power, and for some people, there are many things that are out of their power. Don't believe there are a lot of things in your life that are the result of somebody else to the point that you can't make a change. There are many people that are born into tough situations. Some decide to change their lives and some don't.

SEE YOUR DAY TO THE END

Never be too wrapped up in the past or too caught up in the future. You can only make today beautiful. The past is the only thing that's etched in stone. You can't change it; you can't rewrite it, you can only make today count toward a better future. On the other hand, the future has not come yet, and you're not sure what lies ahead, but you can take action today for the sake of your future. As long as today is still going on, then you must maximize and make optimal use of today's allotted hours. Be sure to live in the days you have and not wish that you were in the days of someone else. Your days are designed for you specifically—specifically for you to develop and move forward.

We all have the same amount of time in a day. The difference between productive days and unproductive days is, of course, what you do in the time allowed. You can never make time longer or shorter, you can, however, be more effective with your time. Some believe that the day is too long. For those people, I say that you haven't experienced living life yet. We must be careful of the time we spend on all the things that demand our attention. All the things that demand our attention can also trample over the small amount of time allowed in one day. New opportunities that are given every day should not be wasted on distractions that come without warning.

Have you ever heard the statement, "Take one day at a time"? I think we all have. This is one of the very few proverbial statements that have become useful in my life. I have many things that I want to achieve in a week's time, a year's time, ten years' time, and even twenty years' time. With all those thoughts going through my head, I am still left with the fact that I can only do my best in the day that I'm living in. For what's to come ten or twenty years from now, I can only plan and work toward it today. Today, right now, is your chance to make your future dreams come true. Say this to yourself, "Only how I use today will I make a better day available to me." Every good year, every good decade, and every good life first started with a day. Your good health will start with the first day you train. A good relationship will start with a day of good communication. There is a significant change that will take place when you begin to initiate what you need to do today. Even though next week or next year has not arrived yet, you will determine it by your use of today. Give today your best. Don't use tomorrow as an excuse to forfeit today. You cannot destroy your today, hoping that tomorrow will be better. You will always give your tomorrow a better chance by preparing for it today. Give today a chance. Common statements such as, "I can't wait for the day to be over," "I know today is going to be hectic," or "I hope I don't see this person today" put you in a position to miss all the good that is available to you every day. New breath, new air, and new relationships are all available in everyday living. Every day, living should have a new meaning to you. Don't just blow with the wind, let the wind excite you to dance. Every moment of every second, allow yourself the pleasure of being optimistic. Besides, it takes more energy to be pessimistic.

Live in the days that you have instead of being angry for the days you don't have. Good and positive changes don't happen because you only hope for them to happen. It happened because you took action, which must start today. If you don't prepare for it today, whatever it is that you're waiting for may never come. Your future has less of a fighting chance when

> *Remember this, later may be too late.*

you do not use today to prepare. Does your future have a chance when you don't use the days you receive to make it great? Probably not. Remember the saying that "It's all in a day's journey." Let your day's journey make the difference it's supposed to make. Starting now, your day can change. A changed day begets a changed week, and a changed week, well, you know the rest. From great days will come great years. Much of your life is in your hands. It shows in the things you have to live with that are the results of your decisions. This is even more true when you decide to live in your greatest

> *If you can focus on the day that you're in with a sense of urgency, you'll accomplish a lot faster. Your future is being created right now, and right now is creating your future.*

days now. Delaying your destiny is one of the worst decisions you could ever make. Remember this, later may be too late. Elderly people have the greatest sense of urgency because of the realization that they are closer to the end of their lives. Younger people are quite the opposite. They believe that life will forever go on the way it is right now. Both have something useful in their approach to life. One possesses a sense of urgency, and the other is only concerned about the day she's living in. If you can focus on the day that you're in with a sense of urgency, you'll accomplish a lot faster. Your future is being created right now, and right now is creating your future. How great your future will be is up to you.

KNOW THAT YOU CAN DO IT

Knowing is different from thinking. Believing in yourself is half the battle of achieving something. Knowing you can do what needs to be done aligns your actions with your thinking. Failure is almost guaranteed to those who are uncertain. When you know that achieving your goals is definite, then that leaves no room for failure. Take the time to listen to your own speech patterns. Do you think you will achieve what you set out to achieve, or do you know it will be done?

People who speak this way give themselves a fifty-fifty chance of succeeding: "It may happen. I'm just going to see what happens. Hopefully, this goes through." Change your choice of words to: "It's going to happen. I will be successful. Nothing will stand in my way." This is the speech pattern of a champion and not of a person who wishes upon a star. Let others doubt you, not you yourself. You will have enough outside doubt, outside unbelief, and outside distractions. Don't increase your struggles by agreeing with the negative outside influences. Give yourself a certainty check. How sure are you about your future? If you're not too sure, you're probably moving slower than you could if you were certain. Moving in fear and doubt will certainly cause you to move haphazardly. And with great fear and doubt comes great slothfulness. You can expedite your next steps in life by no longer doubting the moves you make. Give your stride a boost by moving in confidence. Set yourself apart from the common status quo crowd that never reaches its potential. You can achieve anything that you are sure about. If you are sure that you'll reach your income goals then you won't hesitate to learn what it takes to get there. On the contrary, an uncertain person would reject the information that they need to accomplish their goal. Wavering in your attitude toward success makes it difficult to open your mind to new things. New things could mean new people, new places, new publications to read, or adopting new philosophies that could change your life forever. Know that you will be successful. Know that you will accomplish your goals. Know that you will meet new people and build lasting relationships. Don't underestimate the power of firmly knowing you're just a few steps from what you need to be. Statistics, obstacles, setbacks, and limits have no effect on a person who has the right attitude. In other words, attitude is more important than facts. Our world reflects the results of what can happen if a person has the right attitude versus adapting to what is. "What is" doesn't matter as long as you can believe past what you see. Vision has always surpassed statistics. Hope surmounts reality. A person burdened with purpose doesn't consider failure because it doesn't exist in their world. This doesn't debunk the use of making intelligent and shrewd decisions. This should give you the psychological strength to go forward with your decisions. Intellect is useless without action. Taking calculated action is what makes an intelligent person intelligent. After you give due diligence, don't become over-analytical. Over analyzing anything will make something bigger than what it really is. Break away from being mentally paralyzed by moving in certainty.

Being sure about your decisions has its risks. The number one risk can go without saying, which is that people may be uncertain about your decisions. A great decision is not defined by immediate agreement. The lack of immediate agreement makes having a made-up mind all the more important. People that are drawn to absolute comfort are more common than those that will take a risk. This means the challenges of your decisions may come immediately. I experienced many people making statements to me based on their fear of failure. Statements such as, "Don't take the risk," "Why would you quit your job?" "Play it safe," and the list goes on and on. My first reaction was that these people must want me to fail. The truth is that your desire to succeed can intimidate others. There are people that have given up on their dreams a long time ago. So when you seek to accomplish your dreams, you innately remind others of what they couldn't do. Don't worry; you can't blame yourself for what didn't work out for someone else. Just remember you are just a few steps away from your new life. If you are sure about it, you'll get there a lot quicker.

SLEEP IS FOR LOSERS

Whenever my friends asked me how much sleep I get, I always tell them that sleep is for losers. What I really mean is that too much sleep is never good. You never want to become a sleeper. I've met people who are under thirty years of age that after everything they do, they have to take a nap. Needless to say, they don't get much done. Never give your day away to rest. When you're in motion, stay in motion. Rest is necessary only when it's necessary. For some, sleep is a sport that they play very well.

I will never negate the importance of a good night's rest. Though I will share on the destruction of excessive sleep. Six to eight hours, and eight hours is pushing it, qualifies as enough sleep. This leaves eighteen to sixteen hours a day to run toward your vision. I prefer eighteen hours. A lot can happen in two hours. If you want to achieve something, you must make time for it. Sleep, if you allow it, will take that time. The only thing you do while you're sleeping is breathing. To be more accomplished, you must do more than just breathe. This may sound obvious, but it's not for many. What is even more obvious is that you cannot physically take action at something if you're not awake to do it. Putting yourself in a position to excel can start simply by not being in a position that causes you to fall behind. Remember, we're talking about excessive sleep, not sleep in general. Excessive sleep is only necessary if you need time to hibernate. If you're not hibernating, then there is a demand for you—a demand for you to be at your highest rate of productivity with enough sleep.

PUTTING YOUR DAY TO USE

Never ever give your days away. Every day is too precious for you to spend meeting the wants of everybody else. Stop spending your days doing unimportant favors for friends or unproductive commitments. When the sun rises in the morning, it is for you to see where you're going, not to block your eyes with self-sabotaging habits. Living a life or doing things that are beneficial to others is different than allowing your day to be taken advantage of. Being selfish with your time and talent can make you miserable. Having no control over your day can bring even more misery. The biggest myth is that you can't control anything and that everything just happens. This myth cannot explain the facts that an athlete trains and gets stronger or that a person reads and gets smarter. It doesn't just happen. Preparation plays a major part. Without your day or days of preparation, you could miss an opportunity that was lined up just for you. It is important that when you give portions of your days away for the sake of others, that you have control over the windows of time that you use. Days can come and go so quickly that a conscious effort in how those days are used is a necessity.

> *Real life will teach you to applaud yourself.*

It is easier to go along with the wind than to take authority of your days. Not taking authority over what you have authority of is giving your power to someone else. No one should hold your power in their possession. As long as you neglect what is yours, you leave it up for grabs.

You can never give your responsibilities away. When you make the attempt to, it is still your responsibility. So whether a person succeeds or fails with your responsibilities, the consequences (good or bad) will always follow you. People's health is in disarray because of neglect. Marriages die a slow death because of neglect. And the same is true for your days. If you neglect the precious minutes and hours that you've been given, you can guarantee that failure is at the end.

Schools tend to teach that if you will be good, then someone will always applaud you. Real life will teach you to applaud yourself. Absorb every ounce of enjoyment that comes from retaining every hour that you have in a day.

TAKE YOUR DAY BACK

Who owns your day? The first thing many people would say is "I do." How much of your time do you allow people to use for themselves? After you answer this question, you may come up with a lot of different answers. Your job, your children, the promises you made to other people—we can probably fill your list of the things that steal your time until it's as long as a phone book is thick. So take your day back. Of course, it's easier said than done. At least start the process of getting it done. What parts of your mind or your actions belong to someone else? As you help as many people as you can, never give up your. When others occupy your day for themselves, you slowly but surely become a willing puppet. Puppets are pulled, tugged, and thrown around and are never able to make their own decisions. Unless you could change from a puppet to a living creature like Pinocchio, then being a puppet would not be okay. You cannot leave everything in your life to chance or to the responsibility of someone else. Someone else would never be able to represent who you are internally the way you could.

Taking back your day is also taking back your power and freedom. The words *power* and *freedom* have always sounded good together, and would sound even better when they represent your life. When you take back your days, you obtain the power to fill your days as they ought to be filled—with joy, laughter, productivity, and the things you would like to do. Imagine your day free from nonsense and unnecessary disturbance. Come out of neglectful thinking and into a purposeful rearrangement of your life. You may not be able to control everything; what you can control, you should.

EARN YOUR SLEEP

Challenge each day to be a highly productive day. Your days can be more productive when you sleep less and allow more hours in your day for productivity. I met people who sleep just because they're bored, have nothing to do, claim that they are tired, or habitually sleep far longer than they need. A truly successful person earns their rest. Rest is provided for humans so that they will be energized to do something. The key is to do something after you sleep. For now on, go to sleep with a different mind-set—the mind-set of "I only sleep so that the next day, I can produce more." Before you consider this extreme think of the amount of hours people have been sleeping when they could have spent them producing. It becomes clear that some opportunities will only come if you're available to receive them.

PART TWO:
EVERYTHING IS
NOT WORTH IT

CHAPTER 4:
WHAT MOVES YOUR LIFE FORWARD

GET TO THE GOOD STUFF every day. Don't wait to be who you want to be; be that person now. What's holding you back? Probably nothing is keeping you from achieving your greatest accomplishments. You can give yourself a lot of excuses, truthfully, who really cares about those excuses except for you? You can tell yourself you're too old, you're too fat, you're too black, or you're too white; you can give yourself every excuse imaginable, the truth is that none of them are real obstacles. They're just statements that we, as people, turn into obstacles. You're going to have challenges; I suggest that you don't give yourself more challenges than necessary. I've seen people who weren't so smart who became very intelligent for something they really wanted to accomplish. I watched people who were too short accomplish something that only a tall person should be able to do. I've seen people who were unable become able because they wanted what they wanted bad enough. If you focus on what you can't do and what you don't have, your worst will become all you see in yourself, if you begin to focus on what attributes you have that will move you forward, you will increase in those abilities. Even your skills will begin to, guess what, move forward.

So my question is this: what moves you forward? What keeps you going? What is it that motivates you? What is it that inspires you? What is it that gives you that extra push every single day? Those are the things that you should tap into so that you will propel yourself forward and not wait for somebody to do it for you. When you're trying to figure out what really gets you going, it's best to not worry about what excites someone else. What may excite someone else may not be the same thing that excites you.

So with all that you understand about yourself, what motivates you the most? That's what we want to focus on and begin to channel so that we can bring that to the surface. When your greatest motivations are in front of you, then your level of inspiration will be at an all-time high. When you're greatly inspired, then you're like a lion chasing after an impala. With this level of intense focus and purpose, you'll be doing more than just moving forward, you'll also be moving up. Your chance to become what you always wanted to be is happening right now. After asking myself the question, "What moves me forward?" I came up with some pretty simple answers. Reading moves me forward. Educating myself moves me forward. Exercising moves me forward. Studying moves me forward. Maintaining good relationships moves me forward. These are things that I focus on; everything else is done for the sake of maintaining the things that move me forward. For instance, I will always have multiple responsibilities, but all of my responsibilities do not significantly improve my life. I give my very best to the things that do improve my life significantly. It is important to not spend too many hours in a day just being busy. Being busy will not always result in you moving forward. The same is true when you attempt to do everything as if you can literally do everything. You can try to do everything, or you can just do what's necessary, what's important, and what's valuable for your destiny. Make time for greatness every day. If you're just killing time, doing that will eventually kill you.

DISCOVERING WHAT MOVES YOU FORWARD

Think of this: what has caused your life to propel into a new dimension or what has caused you to go further than what you thought possible? Was it a relationship with someone that moved you ahead? Was it an idea that you presented to the right people, or was it a book or article that you read that changed your perspective on a situation? Whatever it was, if it affected your life in the area of productivity, you should continually do that thing or things. Never do something good just once; if it is that good, you should do it over and over until it loses effect. There have been times in your life when you met the right person, made the right decision, or made the right move. Those things should be done consistently so that your life begins the habitually progress.

Take note of what works for you. If you look at what has brought success in your life, you will figure out how to reproduce those same actions. It may be a time where you gave something your undivided attention. It could be when you finally decided to take a risk. Duplicate what has worked for you so that your successes are not far and few. You can produce more if you do the right things over and over again. What's common is that people do the wrong things over and over again. What is mind-boggling is that those who do the wrong thing over and over again can't figure out why their lives are not what they want them to be. Practicing failure develops big failures. It's that simple. If you don't practice what moves you forward in order to settle for staying comfortable, then you'll get what you practiced and you won't move forward. Don't be afraid to burn the bridges in your life that keep a connection between you and your worst life. Every good tree bears good fruit. If you are doing anything in your life that does not produce good fruit, then that connecting branch much be cut off. Cut it off quickly without any hesitancy. Give patience only to the good things in your life. For some, this may require eliminating a lot of people and things from your immediate circle of friends and activities. These types of great decisions are always followed by great rewards. You can't get the results that you want in your life if the results you don't want are taking up space. Make room for what you want, and if you really want to, you'll make the room. In relationships, it's common that people will keep the person that they're with while hoping for someone better. Someone better may not ever come if you allow dead relationships to stay connected to you. Keeping yourself connected to old things does just that. It keeps you connected to old things—old things such as old mentalities and old speech patterns and old habits are always the enemy of a new life. Be out with the old and in with the new—new things such as new mentalities, new speech patterns, and new and healthy habits. A new life is waiting for you the moment you invite it in. Ask yourself, do I have room enough to invite an entirely new life in—not a partial new life, not a percentage of a new life, an entirely different lifestyle and way of thinking? The closer you move toward your dreams, the closer they move toward you.

> *You can't get the results that you want in your life if the results you don't want are taking up space.*

So only practice what works for you. The options are plentiful when you open your mind to them. What works for you doesn't mean what will work immediately. In other words, many people like to quit on something because they don't see results immediately. That is called quitting way too soon. Whatever you do, using ethics, morals, and intelligence will always work. Simple ethics work. An honest person never has to look over their shoulder while being afraid of a lie catching up to them. A person of morals is not consumed with what relationship he will take advantage of next. When you practice ethics, morals, and intellect, you expedite success. Practicing these things positions you perpetually for the best relationships in every area of your life. When you utilize integrity, moving forward with only have slight interruptions.

Figuring out what moves you forward is not the hard part; maintaining the discipline to keep moving forward is. Adapt yourself to opening up and accepting the challenges that act as checkpoints to the next chapters in your life. There is no challenge, fight, or fear that can stop you completely. Their purposes are to prepare and propel you forward. Don't avoid the things in your life that move you forward because they may present a challenge. Where there is a challenge, there is a chance. When you are open to challenges, you are open to the chance to move forward.

DOING WHAT MOVES YOU FORWARD

There is a possibility that you may not be progressing at the rate that you could be. Making things easier for yourself so that you feel no resistance will cause you to move backward. It is the same as a person being in a gym for two hours and never breaking a sweat. Being at a playground with your children would have been a better use of time. Just doing something doesn't mean you're moving forward.

I've heard this expression a million times: "You have to start small." You will always start smaller than where you'll end up. This doesn't mean that you start beneath where you already are. Out of ignorance, people are told to take this route in order to be humble. If you're able to start at level five, don't start at level two believing that you're taking the right path of starting small. Begin at the level you're on.

Out of a fear of failure, taking the easiest path provides a convenience for fear. If your life is full of convenience, then you become lazy (I think we all know the results of lazy people). The lazy mentality seeks to be handed everything. Having this mentality is okay if you expect to have later in life only what you have now. If you want more, then having a lazy mentality is not the way to go. Laziness consists of waiting for someone to do something for you and hoping that they do it just right to make your life easier. If you pay for services, this should be expected, this should not be expected in the development of your life. In life, there are no magic wands, genie bottles, or lucky coins that actually work. A rabbit's foot or lucky underwear won't make it happen. The difference will be made by you. Your choice of people, places, and things will all shape a certain kind of life. Will your choices create the kind of life you want? If so, then change your decisions. You can easily complain to yourself by saying it's not that easy. But living with the results of bad decisions is not that easy either. Cultivate and mold the life you want by cultivating and molding your mind. You transform your mind by continually introducing it to the life you want. If you want more money, introduce your mind to financial literacy. If you want more friends, introduce your mind to what attracts good people. If you want better health, introduce your mind to a disciplined lifestyle. Your mind is waiting to be introduced to the things you want. Make no assumptions about whether or not you're moving forward. For if you assume you are doing something, you probably aren't. Be absolutely sure that you're moving forward by periodically calculating the results of your actions. If you're disappointed at the results, you can change your actions. You already possess the intelligence to do so. Think of something that you pursued in your life. It could be a woman, a man, a job, a college degree, or someone's approval. If it didn't work the first time, you reevaluated your approach and went for it again. This same strategic evaluation is used in accomplishing anything. Simply, if you fail, figure out why you failed and don't repeat what caused the failure.

> *You can easily complain to yourself by saying it's not that easy. But living with the results of bad decisions is not that easy either.*

CHANGE PRIORITIES TO WIN

If you still give time-killers, energy-killers, and dream-killers the priority in your life, then you can't win at anything. The best way to view or understand what your priorities are is to look at your bank account. When you look at your bank account, you'll see what your priorities really are. That's why a budget never works unless you have proper priorities. Budgets don't change priorities; they just give you an idea of things that you can focus on. When you look at your bank account, you will see the things that you consider before anything else. You will also see what habits you hold on to. What you believe is important to you, you'll always be its financial constituent. If you can change your priorities, you can change your spending or investing habits as well as everything else in your life. Priorities are what give your mind and heart and body their initiatives. Simply changing your priorities will change your heart's desires, your mind's focuses, and your body's intentions. Your top priority with money should be investing to grow your wealth, your top priority with your body should be health, your top priority in your relationships should be growth, and your top priority in your businesses should be productivity. Once your priorities are in the right place, then expect your life to get into place as well. You can only do what your priorities allow you to do. So by changing your priorities, you allow yourself to do, more or less, the right thing.

WHAT GETS YOU GOING, NOT WHAT OTHERS PUSHED ON YOU

I had a friend who went to college simply because her parents told her to; when she was done, she was very upset, angry and unsure of what to do with her life. Believe it or not, this is typical amongst college graduates. Even more true is the fact that people live their entire lives in pursuit of some dream, goal, or desire that someone else put on them. A friend may have told you to choose this career because that's where the money is. A professor may have suggested a job to you to build your résumé. These things are helpful, though you shouldn't build a life around suggested advice. Fulfillment comes from within; no one can fill your internal cup except for you. So what do you want? Not what mommy, uncle, father, friend, spouse, coworker, teacher, or professor wants for you, but what do you want for yourself? To go deeper into this question that you asked yourself, take money out of the equation. Don't want something because it may get you a lot of money or recognition, only want what will fulfill you and put a smile on your face every morning you wake up.

THE RIGHT PROBLEM/ MR. PROBLEM

Moving forward is simple yet challenging. It is taking the paths that you have avoided and are afraid of that presents challenges. As humans, we tend to complicate matters that are relatively simple. A forward-progressing life means just that, moving forward and progressing. When taking the path of least resistance, there's not too many complications. Matters are complicated when the path is not so easy. Complaints, murmuring, and the feeling of utter defeat can come after the realization that something may not be so easy. Be opposite of this truth. Become excited about difficult matters. Out of a difficult matter will develop uncommon wisdom. Common wisdom is the result of going through common circumstances. The greater the uniqueness of your situation, (and you will be faced with very unique situations) the greater the uniqueness of your wisdom. Walking away from problems means you are walking away from discovering solutions that can change your life and the lives of others. Your destiny can get a jump-start when you face the right problem.

Could you believe it? To get ahead in your life, all you need is the right problem to solve. Imagine that, the right problem. I know this is a strange statement to make, but nothing could be closer to the truth. You will always be needed where you are the best solution to the problem, and your new ideas are hidden in difficult situations. Think of something very challenging that you have faced in the past, that you could not see an end to. After the issue is resolved and over with, you are then able to look back and realize what you were really made of. The right problem brought you to the right perspective. Now if you face similar problems, they're a piece of cake. With this in mind, there's no telling what you can do as long as you face your problems. Your new life, your desired relationships, and your total makeover could be right in front of you with the appearance of a problem at the door to greet you. You should shake his hand and prepare to fight Mr. Problem. He will do his job of working against you. You must do your job by not just working against him, but also by creating a solution that leaves him defenseless.

WHAT MOVES YOU BACKWARD

Whatever you allow to move you backward has the potential to do just that. Entertainment can be healthy, so relax, kick back, or take some time off work. On the contrary, excessive entertainment hinders you from doing the things that really matter. Doing good repeatedly makes for a great person or personality; when you do good once in a blue moon, you don't develop at all. Every day you should be learning something new. When days pass and you realize you have not grown in education and knowledge, you are doing something wrong. If you're not using what you already have, you are simply moving backward. Every day people are getting smarter, becoming stronger, and developing new skills and talents; you should be one of them. You should always be on the right side of progress.

> *Excessive entertainment hinders you from doing the things that really matter.*

THERE'S NO STANDING STILL

In life, there are only two directions a person can go—forward or backward; there's no in between. Even when you go through a transition, you are moving forward. Too often, an average person believes that not doing anything is equal to being in a standstill position. Like a three-dollar bill, this is a figment of a person's imagination. When you're standing still, you're not being challenged, your mind is not active, and your body deteriorates—thus moving you backward. Moving toward challenges, obstacles, and oppositions is a sign of progress. Never take a setback as a sign of moving backward. Sometimes it takes a little opposition to spearhead you forward. Learn to analyze when you are moving backward or if you're going through transition. Transition is when you're being prepared to move forward even though it feels like nothing is going on. The preparation and development that takes place during your personal transition is always necessary if you want an explosive progression.

USE YOUR DIFFICULTIES

Whenever you start something there's always an extra boost that's needed. Never confuse the difficulty of starting as the reason to never start. Everything will never be just right in order for you to start moving forward. So, you just need to start and start quickly. As you move forward, you begin to build up momentum, and as you build momentum, you gain the strength to let go of things that stop you from moving forward. Kick, scream, push, pull, tug—do whatever it takes to get yourself going. Whatever you do, just get going. I am oftentimes faced with the struggle of getting started when dealing with something new. A new project to complete, a new book to read, or a new exercise regimen all can present the obstacle or hurdle of starting a new initiative. The good news is that when faced with something new, there's always the possibility of a new opportunity, new understanding, new wisdom, and new strength. Use your difficulty the same way you would use resistance bands to build your strength. Every difficulty will help you if you are willing to stay in the fight of changing your life.

Never confuse the difficulty of starting as the reason to never start.

No problem that you face is too big or difficulty so complicated that creativity can't compress and demystify.

IT GETS EASIER AS YOU GO

Only after an athlete has trained for some time does he or she feel the ease of certain regiments and drills. The same is true for anything else in life.

After you've done something a few times, it gets easier. This is a statement of fact, the truth of which is not discovered unless you actually take action. Becoming great and overcoming something that is difficult are really just a few practices away. Step by step, action by action, and risk by risk, you become a greater, stronger, and better version of you. If that be the case, you should never set goals that are low. Set them high enough to improve yourself. The higher your goals, the greater you become. The higher your goals, the more you stretch and reach to your fullest potential.

Prepare to Lose as You Gain

Everyone seeks to gain—whether the gains are profits, influences, connections, or new friends. To gain more, you'll outgrow some things. Over the years, I've gained extensive knowledge relating to investments, businesses, and people. To gain that knowledge and awareness, I've had to lose old information. Losing is not always bad—especially when you're gaining from it. I've lost friends to gain much better friends. I've lost employees to gain much better employees. I've even quit many jobs in pursuit of my destiny. Life and money are not similar in loss and gains. When money is lost, it's lost. Life's losses, however, can turn into extraordinary gains. Your personal wisdom, understanding, strength, and tolerance level can all change due to losses in your life.

Future losses may not be planned, though at times will become necessary. There are things that I planned never to give up, but my future didn't allow me to keep them. When your life is moving forward, there are some habits that you'll be forced to give up—habits that you may have not considered bad at all. The amount of TV, parties, or gatherings will come to be less of a priority. Losing something that you kept in your life for years is not a bad thing if it releases you to go further in life. Philosophies that you thought were right will turn out to be wrong if they contradict the forward progress in your life. Who knows what you may have to do away with, because who knows the feats

> *Losing something that you kept in your life for years is not a bad thing if it releases you to go further in life.*

that you may accomplish? The greater your accomplishments, the greater the process of elimination.

When you clean your house, you may expect to straighten some things up and wipe some things down. When you expect to thoroughly clean your house, it will require you to lift couches and beds, move furniture from corners, and stand on ladders to clean high places. By the time you're done, you will have thrown away a lot more things than you anticipated. It's not a bad thing that you have bags full of trash. It is an excellent thing that you got rid of so many things that you don't need. This is exactly what happens when you take step after step in the direction of your goals. Your tolerance level will drop for the things you thought you needed, and you will begin only to tolerate what you do need. You'll begin to realize people who have held you back. You'll start to habitually eliminate the waste in your life. Nonsense will lose its appeal to you. This is all the result of progress. The benefit of wanting a good life is that you'll be encouraged to live a better life. This is not a lesson of stubbornness. On the contrary, this is a sign of selectiveness.

CHAPTER 5:
DO WHAT'S IMPORTANT

LET ME BE VERY STRAIGHTFORWARD when I say everything is not important. Answering every social media message and text is not as important as writing your book. Making sure that you satisfy every wish and need of everybody you know is not as important as moving or growing your business. Let's put things in perspective. Everything cannot be at the same level of importance in your life; there are some things that are musts. It must be done, it must be focused on, and it must have your attention. Then there are some things that are not important and that you should just do whenever you feel like doing them. What's important to you may be different than what's important to somebody else. For me, I put a high priority on studying; for other people, it may be a waste of time. I put a high priority on things in my life that will help me grow as an individual. For some people, personal growth is the farthest thing from their mind. I have been crucified for placing a very high importance on building my businesses before they existed instead of getting a job. In life, some things you will have to see as important no matter who may agree with you. Remember, nobody else will have the vision for your life; nobody else will have the vision for your businesses or for your plans of success, so you must make sure that you know what's important for you before anybody else attempts to make that decision for you. For me, maintaining my integrity is very important; for other people that I've run across, it just seems to be boring. To this day, I have the best time in my life because when I do have fun, I never have to worry about things from my past coming back to haunt me.

True importance is in the eyes of the beholder. It is in the eyes of the person who has their priorities intact and who knows what needs to be done. You cannot allow people to give you your importance or priorities for you. You must make these kinds of decisions for yourself. For me, my health is very important. To be able to run, jump, lift, and stretch means the world to me. Due to traveling and a list of different responsibilities, I must have the body that's ready to do anything and everything at any given moment. Because I have made my health one of the greater, more important things in my life, it forces me to make different decisions in other areas. That's the power of knowing what's important to you. If your spouse is important to you, then you will not cheat. If your health is important to you, junk food becomes less appealing. When your business is very important to you, every choice you make relating to your business is made with a lot more vigilance. Determining what's important to you forces you to act differently, spend your money differently, be different, and think differently. Constantly considering how your actions will affect you and others will significantly change your way of living for the better. The best way to figure out what's important to you is by really thinking about what would make the greatest impact on your life and other people's lives. If it will just affect you, it's probably not that important. So ask yourself what it is that you will do. What is it that you will study? What product, what service, or what thing will you develop in your life that will have the greatest impact on other people's lives? If you can answer these questions, then you can change your life and the world.

WHAT'S IMPORTANT

A little while ago I had the time to narrow down the things that are most important to me and my development. Things that help me maintain good relationships, provide me access to more capital to pursue ventures, and things that help me produce ideas and creativity. You could be a CEO of a public corporation, a stay-at-home mom, a janitor, a teacher—whatever it may be, there are things that will help you succeed. Whatever they are, focus on those things and perfect them. So what's important to you? It may not be the same for you as it is for everybody else. This requires an honest analysis of your own life without the influence of naysayers, doubters, and people who don't have the same vision for you as you do. If you are a teacher, one of the things that may be important to you could be making creative outlines for lessons, increasing student participation, and motivating students to come to class consistently. If you are an entrepreneur, your focuses may be to raise capital, manage people well, and increase your influence. The core focuses are different things for different people and are according to their professions, goals, and life purposes.

SOME THINGS ARE UNIMPORTANT

The hardest part of realizing that something is unimportant in your life is for it to be something you enjoy more than anything. Too much of an unimportant thing will keep you active but will not satisfy you in the long run. I'm not suggesting that you shouldn't have a good time. No life should be filled with just work and no play. A huge imbalance occurs when 5 percent of your time is used for work and 95 percent of your time is used for play. This is common when a person would rather be distracted with unimportant things than face life. You'll never get the full experience of life if you run from it. Even though life's

> *Too much of an unimportant thing will keep you active but will not satisfy you in the long run.*

challenges can feel hard to bear, there are many pleasures to enjoy as you overcome each obstacle. What can be a pivotal point in your life is a simple confession to yourself of what needs to be done versus only considering what can provide you a good time with fabricated benefits.

Some things are just not worth the majority of your time. Apply your health, intelligence, and strength to the things that will contribute to the greater good. When you're focused on helping someone else and using what you have available, you'll be more motivated and willing to stay consistent. This will give your life more meaning, and you'll wake up more energetic. Only fear will cause you to avoid the great things you can do by indulging only in what will entertain you. Sadly enough, many people would rather keep their heads down and occupied with wasteful behavior than to experience the greatest life they could ever live. Avoiding life's greatest experiences will create much regret and disappointment. Explore the different options that are made available to you every day by indulging in the things that are important to your life's purpose. Do the things that complement your interests and strengths. Studying, reading, and writing are not things that are just designated for students in a school, it is also for anybody who understands the importance of building themselves. Desiring more for yourself is an honorable thing. What's even more honorable is desiring the best for other people. Immediately begin the process of eliminating some unimportant things from your life.

Excessive downtime, thirteen hours of sleep a day, and excessive partying are just some of the things that can destroy what could be a beautiful life. A focused and productive life leads to focused and productive activities. One success begets another success, and the domino effect begins. Success is very contagious, and as you change your life, you will compel others to change their lives as well. Once you start this journey, you will no longer tolerate what used to hold you back.

WHAT NEEDS YOUR ATTENTION

Being a good steward, to some, is giving every single thing your undivided attention. Nothing could be more further from the truth. Every single thing in your life does not deserve your undivided attention 100 percent of the time. Actually, if you narrow down things in your life from the most important to the least important and give the most important things your undivided attention, then you'll become more productive. Life is too short for you to spend your time on everything. Be detail oriented when it comes to the important stuff. Who cares about all the bad news that is easily found or heard on a daily basis? What purpose do gossip, "he-said, she-said," pessimistic opinions, or unenthusiastic people have in your life? Take the time to comb through your life and figure out what needs to be there and what doesn't. You'll be amazed, if you're honest with yourself, on how many things need to be eliminated from your life, how many habits are killing you, and what changes need to be made. People who are regretful and angry in their later years of life didn't just get there in one day. It took years of habits and actions to get to a life ending in failure. If your life hasn't ended, you still have a chance. You can eliminate a lot of those years of failure by eliminating what's unimportant in your life right now. Don't become an expert bag lady who drags old and useless things into new chapters of their life. Don't be afraid to be free from what you don't need.

DON'T STICK TO UNIMPORTANT THINGS

Once you identify the things that are not important, don't stick to them. Only a fool would take the time out to realize what's not important and then do nothing about it. Over-analytical people analyze things, people, and situations, only never to do anything about it and to continue in their analysis. Literally detach yourself from what is and who is unimportant for your destiny. Why choose to stick to what doesn't work and what hasn't worked? Calling someone "unimportant" can sound harsh. What I am relating to you is that people are important, still there are some that have no reason to be connected to you. They don't help you, and you don't help them, which makes for an unhealthy relationship.

The important things to you should serve a purpose. They should give life to your goals and to the plans that you have to achieve those goals. Unimportant things do just the opposite. They keep you busy; they can even be entertaining, they still serve no purpose. Self-reevaluation is something that we all should do. If you take a holistic snapshot of your life, you may find things that have lingered around for years and do not serve any purpose for you. Ask yourself the question: "What do I need from this habit, relationship, associate, or associations?" If you have to think long and hard or you just have to make up something to justify its existence in your life, then it may be time to let it go. Letting go of something can be hard, but the benefits are priceless. You can never put a dollar amount on you fulfilling your life by eliminating unimportant things. There is a belief that things can hold on to you and never let you go. I have found most commonly that people hold on to things and never let them go. Only people could hold on to the past, a failed endeavor, or a bad situation. None of these things have the ability to hold on to people because they themselves do not have arms to do so. Allow yourself to breathe again by cutting off the things that steal your oxygen. Be determined that you will never lose another thing due to poor vigilance. You wouldn't open the door for a thief to come into your house.

Our lives are designed to increase and prosper. It is hard for anything to increase if there is a constant barrier. Each time you do not do away with unimportant relationships, habits, etc., you create a self-imposed barrier. When you eliminate the unimportant things, you eliminate a barrier. Barriers are not a sign of defeat, they are chances to evaluate what needs to be done away with. As quickly as you create a barrier, you can tear it down. No barrier in life is to be permanent unless you allow it to be. So what's the unimportant stuff? The unimportant stuff is barrier-creators, life-stealers, and time-wasters. Get rid of these things quickly because your life is counting on it.

THE "I MUSTS" ARE DIFFERENT THAN THE "TO-DOS"

At some point or another, we all have accumulated a to-do list. On average, most people go from one to-do list to another to-do list to another to-do list only to find themselves more busy, never accomplishing anything.

No matter how long, planned-out, or how extensive our to-do lists are, we really only accomplish what we feel we must accomplish. As soon as "I must" is in front of a statement, it's more than likely going to be done. A to-do list is necessary for small, forgettable things. Life goals and things you feel that you must accomplish are usually backed up by your emotions and zeal. When your zeal and emotions are attached to a thing, writing it down becomes unnecessary because you already have the attitude to get it done. You never need to write down when to take a shower, when to use the bathroom, or when to love your children because these are "must-dos". Whatever you want to accomplish has to become a "must-do", right now. Doing this is foreign to people who are passive and over-patient. A widely accepted theory is that it will take an exceptional amount of time to achieve your goals. It will take time; you can decide to decrease that time by relentlessly pursuing worthy goals. Whatever you want to achieve in life, make a daily habit of declaring to yourself, "I must," followed by whatever your goals are.

Believe in What's Important to You

When you are different, you will be criticized, sneered at, and questioned. And one of the things that people have questioned me about the most is why I spend so much time on certain things. The answer is easy: they're important to me. I spend money on what's important to me. I educate myself on what's important to me, and I focus on the things that are important to me, even if they may not be important to the people around me. When you have adopted a winning and productive philosophy, what's important to you begins to change even though it may not change instantly for the people around you. When you go from consumer to investor, you no longer meditate on ways to spend your money, rather on how to make it multiply. When you go from single to married, your priorities become less selfish. No matter what the transformation, your important priorities tend to change very swiftly. After reading this book, you may go from time-waster to a productive user of time. You may even go from feeling insignificant to realizing you're important. With transformation comes a change of heart, a change of mind, and a change of activities.

Life responsibilities can sometimes get the best of many of us. It can cause you to push life-changing priorities to the side to take care of immediate financial or family obligations. Although obligations are necessary and may require some of your attention, they should never supersede your major goals. As long as you tend to only you and your family, you will remain unfulfilled. True fulfillment comes when you serve a greater cause than your household. With that being said, a lot of what you do and focus on should benefit those outside of your home. Focus your attention on making a great contribution to society—not just your local society, your society abroad as well. You'll be amazed at how many problems in this world that you possess the best solution for.

CHAPTER 6:
WASTE, IT'S FOR TRASH CANS

ARE YOU A DOORMAT? NO, I didn't think so. So why tolerate the daily waste, trash, and junk that land on your life and stay there as if you were a doormat? I wonder how much trash has been in your life for so long that it began to blend in and began to look like you and almost took the form of you. Could it be more productive not to do more but to actually get rid of more junk, get rid of more trash, and get rid of more waste in your life so that you'll be freed up to actually do the important things? Put the waste and the junk in your life where they belong: in the trash—not in your mind, not in your heart, and not in your spirit. Just throw it away and be done with it forever. Can you imagine a life that has done away with junk that you have carried around for years? Can you imagine it being gone forever? Forever is a pretty long time to be done with something; *forever* means "I will never go back to something." That's the power of throwing away waste.

WHAT GOES IN THE TRASH

Stuff that stinks or what is simply not clean anymore usually goes in the trash. Things from which you have gotten all their use should go in the trash. Old, outdated, useless products generally go to the trash. The only time these things are not put in the trash is if they are in the possession of a hoarder. Hoarders have a problem with letting go of old things. A person would then have to ask the question, if hoarders are so afraid of new things, how do they accumulate so much? Well, just because it's new to them, doesn't mean it's new. Hoarders tend to accumulate lots of old, useless, worthless items just to feel some level of security. Now ask yourself, have you become a hoarder in life? Do you leave old friends just to acquire the same type of person in new-friend form? Do you go from dead-end career to another dead-end career? Have you not yet thrown away the old and dead philosophies, views, thoughts, and actions that keep you in the same life? Too many people try the same things every single day while still expecting something different. They have the same speech patterns, and they expect their lives to gain some different result. Have you ever told yourself, "My situation stinks"? Well, it's probably because you have a lot of trash in it. Trash stinks, and if you want the smell to leave, you have to throw the trash out. Even things that smell good wouldn't catch your attention if they're surrounded with trash. No feeling can replace what it feels like to be detached from the waste in your life. When I organize my office, I think of these two things: anything that is important, I can find a place for, and if I can't find a place for it, to the trash it goes. All the out-of-place things in your life, put them in their place, and if they don't have a place, then more than likely they need to be thrown away.

DUMP THE TRASH IN YOUR LIFE

It is inevitable that where there is production, there will also be waste. Factories produce goods as well as waste. Even a car can't get you across town without producing waste. In one day, you can make important phone calls, have meetings, play with your kids, and by the time you finish, you will have many things to throw away. Waste comes with productivity, so it is important that you develop a system to dispose of waste quickly. Take a look at your e-mail inbox and social media messages to get an idea as to how fast things can accumulate in your life. Message after message and post after post can even be a little overwhelming.

Take the time to detox internally and externally. Before attempting to get organized, you have a better shot at just throwing away all the things you don't need. Trash can be very sneaky in how it shows up. Before you know it, your house can be in disarray, there's old food under your car seat, and your mind is thinking one million thoughts a minute. This is the result of clutter and calamity. Having a stress-free life is achievable by detaching yourself from things that apply strain to you.

Where does the trash in your life come from? Well, only you would know. Most houses that I've been to, big or small, have their largest trash can in the kitchen. This is common because that's where most of the trash is accumulating. If the trash is not disposed of quickly, then it will attract even more trash and rodents. If it's disposed of quickly, then it'll makes for a better home. For the sake of getting rid of trash in your life, see that your life is one big house. Pinpoint what part of your life accumulates the most trash so that you can prepare yourself to dispose of it quicker than other areas in your life. This will eliminate the risk of a stinky life and attracting more of what you don't want. No one likes junk, even though the average person has more garbage in his life than he can handle. Trash causes psychological and even physical dilemmas. If your mind is full of wasteful thoughts, then it will cause your body to take wasteful actions.

Old Doesn't Always Mean Trash

It is said that if you're old-fashioned, your ways might be outdated. But what's true is that a lot of the old-fashioned ways pertaining to relationships and entrepreneurship are what many of us are still living off of today.

Values, morals, and virtues are never to be thrown away. If things such as morals and virtues have made it through the years and have lasted through the ages, then they must work. They shouldn't be classified as old-fashioned.

It is never old-fashioned to not lie, steal, and cheat in business. It is never old-fashioned to chase after your goals and dreams no matter your age or the obstacles that may lie ahead. It is never old-fashioned or outdated to think independently and go against the naysayers. Never consider what works as being old-fashioned.

Can I Avoid Waste/Trash?

Waste and trash are often unavoidable. Even productivity sometimes can produce waste. Your best chance is to make sure it is disposed of quickly. Comb through your life many times and distinguish between what is useful and what is not useful. As the unuseful things show up again, you'll be able to dispose of them quickly. After you clean once, you have to clean again; that's just life. With every new cleaning comes a new lesson.

As a result of never having enough, a person maybe afraid to let go of what they have even if it's not helpful. So they keep people, places, and things around that have lost their use a long time ago and will convince themselves they need them to feel secure. There is no security in false security. Holding on to junk will only make you and your life messy.

Are you attracted to mess? Having a lot of it is the equivalent of having nothing.

WHOSE FAULT IS IT?

The instant you point your finger at someone else, you literally release your own power over your own life to someone else. No matter your situation, whosever fault it is, if it's your responsibility, then you have to make changes.

To accomplish any goal, start in steps. After you look at your project holistically, break it down into accomplishable steps. Look at your giant limb by limb to see how easy it is to make a giant fall to its knees. Large businesses are combinations of small businesses. Books are just combinations of words. Humans are just a combination of matter. If you put it all together, you have one great thing. It is the same with issues that you're facing. Big problems are just a combination of little problems; large piles of trash are just a combination of pieces of trash. If you attack your large problems in small steps, eventually the problems can be eliminated. Debt, obesity, failed relationships, and other problems in general all started with small seeds. With the same principles we used to build our problems, we can use those to eliminate our problems—which is one step at a time.

PART THREE:
MAKE PEOPLE
BELIEVE YOU

Chapter 7:
Who You Really Are Is Really Who People Get

PHONIES ARE A DIME A dozen. It is not wise to spend an excessive amount of time focusing on your surface level issue. It is very smart to focus the majority of your energy on your core instead of how you look, how you dress, and how you act in public. Your core represents who you really are. Every action and every word you speak will follow who you really are. Be genuine and you never have to remember your lines wherever you go; you can just be you. I promise you that life is simpler this way; life becomes easier when you are genuine and not forced to put on a facade that is based on where you are at the time. Actors are only believable to those who want to believe them. A person may be able to trick herself into believing her act though that most definitely doesn't mean she tricks everyone else. Who you really are can never be faked. If who you are is not who you want to be, just remember that who you are is not ordained and can be changed through intentional effort.

> It is important that you develop the type of core that is filled with good stuff so that when people dig deeper into your mind, into your heart, and into who you really are, they will find better instead being disappointed.

Give yourself the chance to be honest with yourself. Be truthful with yourself and analyze yourself to realize what needs to be changed and what needs to be improved upon. When I visit social network websites, I always run across a picture that makes a person look very nice until that picture is expanded. I have been utterly shocked and amazed at what a difference expanding a picture can make. When the picture is small and at a distance, everything is fine. When the picture is close-up and you can see details, then the feeling of being misled comes upon you. This should not be a replica of your life. It is important that you develop the type of core that is filled with good stuff so that when people dig deeper into your mind, into your heart, and into who you really are, they will find better instead being disappointed.

WHAT'S YOUR CORE PHILOSOPHY?

You can easily figure out what your core philosophy is by your daily actions, how you pursue goals, and the people that you keep around you. When you analyze these things, you will see what you truly believe in and what is at the core of your belief system. A person can only really transform when there is a transformation at their core. Even when you learn something new, it is only new information to your mind until it is practiced enough to become a part of your core. The only way something can enter into your core is by continually doing it until it becomes a habit. Whatever you want to become focused on, place those characteristics into your core until they become who you are. You are not far away from becoming everything you want to be just as long as you develop the right habits.

IT'S BETTER NOT TO REMEMBER YOUR LINES

When you're a different person everywhere you go, you have to remember your scripts, your lines, and which character you are at the time. Nothing could be more exhausting than this. My suggestion is that you should be honest and sincere. It is an actor's job to pretend to be something that he is not. To practice this in your own life will cause an array of confusion. You will be known for something you are not. Have enough courage to be consistent in your character and personality. You'll be amazed at the ease that is created when you become consistent. People will become very disappointed in you if they fall in love with a character that you perpetrated and not you. No one likes a fraud.

See your life as one life, not many different lives.

Too often people make up themselves to camouflage who they really are and expect great results. If this is practiced continually, then in a very short time, you will have dressed up as many different characters that you will not be able to keep up with. If you live a life in which you spread yourself thin, then you leave yourself with no energy to do anything substantial. I understand presentation and professionalism, however lying doesn't justify the two.

People are attracted to genuineness. A genuine person can be tested by anyone, and what will be found is more genuineness. Remember, it's a small world, and who you are will quickly get around. This is no worry to an honest person who maintains integrity. To the scammers and soothsayers, their end is always near. What's even better is surrounding yourself with people who symbolize where you want to be and the characteristics you would like to embrace. See your life as one life, not many different lives. School, work, sports, business—whichever of these are in your life must connect at some point. And the points where they connect are usually in the areas of character and integrity. Maintaining these two areas make for a whole life and not a broken one. Sure, one part of your life may need more energy, such as studying or times out of your day to think to yourself. Just keep this in mind that every part of your life connects to make your life what it is. By separating parts of your life as being totally different, you'll force more energy to be lost. Connecting your life will help you maintain a greater focus and energy and you will jump-start the different parts of your life by giving them the attention they need.

> *Seven lives are for seven people, not one person.*

If you wear seven hats, then it is not smart to divide your life into seven separate lives. Seven lives are for seven people, not one person. One life is for one person. Consolidate your life by being one person for your one life. Becoming seven different people would make you bipolar and unstable. You create stability for yourself the moment you decide to be one person. That's all you need to be—one person. Instantly you'll be released from the stress and the worry that's associated with having multiple counterparts. You will always get a lot more done as one person than you could as many different people. Just like when you hit the refresh button on a computer to help it function better, refresh yourself!

YOUR FLAWS ARE NOT PERMANENT

An old and a young dog can always be taught new tricks. What makes something permanent is that it can't be changed. You and everything about you, no matter your age, can be changed. If you don't like your weight, change it; if you don't like your speech patterns, change them. If you just grow accustomed to something, that doesn't mean it can't be changed. Every weakness you have can be turned into strengths. Your greatest shortcoming could be your greatest testimony. Your deepest failure could be your greatest strength. Let only the good things in your life become permanent by maintaining them. Something can only be permanent if it is nurtured. Begin to nurture your talent and your abilities to create the person you always wanted to be.

What is it that you really want to change? Who is it that you would really like to connect with? Whatever's stopping you more than likely is not permanent. A permanent marker stain cannot be washed, rearranged, or even melted away. Still, your habits and daily activities can be cleaned up and rearranged to your liking.

YOU REALLY SHOULD BE YOURSELF

The idea to pretend you're something that you're not in order to get ahead is ridiculous. What other person could you be besides yourself? I admit there will be some things about you that will have to change, but your uniqueness should never change.

Consistency is your best weapon in building great relationships, and especially a reputation. Who you are, no matter the bad or good times, is who you really are and who people will view you as.

A person with false character does what's right until she gets what she wants. More often than not, this type of character fails in consistency and durability. Honesty and integrity have become characteristics that are viewed as amazing because few people have them. I say, when you find good people keep them around you for as long as you can. Never take quality people for granted because they will inspire good habits to come out of you. Good character is essential to life, business, and relationships. It is much easier to cheat, steal, lie, and manipulate to get ahead. With this ease comes a great price. Millionaires have become broke due to unethical practices. Beautiful relationships have been destroyed through dishonesty. Immorality has never worked and it never will. It is important that you maintain great character for you and not for people. Maintaining good character—great character—for you

> *The idea to pretend you're something that you're not in order to get ahead is ridiculous.*

is important because it may not always be applauded by people. People will love to do business with you because of your honesty, but it probably won't get you a trophy. You must take pleasure in good character, for is not the most appreciated thing.

> *I admit there will be some things about you that will have to change, but your uniqueness should never change.*

SECRETLY CHANGE (IF YOU DO IT PRIVATELY, YOU'LL DO IT PUBLICLY)

Every secret thing that you do will eventually come out. It is inevitable that the character and personality that you have will eventually be recognized by everyone you encounter. You can only fake it for so long, and then the real you comes out. So whoever you want people to see you as, be that person privately. The human race is not fooled by pretenders. Humans have been around for too long for any new type of phony to go over people's heads. The principle is simple: whoever I really want to be and how I want people to perceive me, I must become that person in private quarters. Alone time can be the best time to reevaluate yourself and see what needs to be improved. You can even deal with a crowd much better when you deal with the crowd of thoughts in your mind. Don't ever be afraid of the alone times that you have, because they could be some of the most important times in your life. Being away from the crowd can give you a different perspective on life. Being away from outward influences and the noises of life can help your spirit to calm and your mind to relax.

A great athlete displays his daily training habits when he performs in front of crowds. Think about it, first come training, then comes the performance. Your private life is your training and your public life, for lack of a better term, is the performance. Whatever you practice is what you'll display. You cannot be in public what you refuse to be in private. Reorganizing your private quarters to create an atmosphere that produces what you want to be, is a great start to a better you. The sky is the limit when you realize applying simple principles to your life can create an extraordinary life, the kind of life you'll be pleased with.

Chapter 8:
Be Worth It

IF YOU WANT A HIGHER pay, you must be more valuable to the marketplace. If you want a greater attraction from your spouse, you must increase in value to him or her. Whatever you want out of life you can have, as long as you increase your value enough to attract it. Just because you're valuable somewhere, doesn't mean you're valuable everywhere. I am not asking you to become a people-pleaser or butt-kisser. I am telling you that prosperity comes to those who are able to provide value to others. When you can give increasing value to others, then you become sought-after and not a kiss-up. Much is given to a person who knows how to provide a lot of the right things. The right things could be advice, products or services, or whatever it is that adds increasing value to someone's life. Whatever good you possess, give lots of it and your rewards will be immeasurable.

Believing that you deserve what you have not earned is the mentality of a spoiled child. Whatever you want in life, just position yourself for it. You can be the type of person that doesn't just dream of what can happen, but decides to makes it happen.

Being worth it means being worth what you're asking for. Is it time, money, conversation, or whatever you deem as what you want? I heard Charlie Munger state that the safest way to get what you want is to deserve what you want. It's so simple; it is the golden rule, so to speak. Whatever it is that you want, have you become worth it? Never become angry again for feeling that you deserve something that you have not become worthy of. Anyone can become worthy of anything. To you I ask have you become worthy of what you have desired? If you haven't, it is all in the matter of becoming worthy of what you want.

YOU CAN BECOME ANYTHING

Remember, anything is possible—even in your life. You will never be limited by your education, the people you know, or the resources you don't have because all these things can be acquired. Your road to becoming who and what you want to be, starts with a simple choice. If you decide to do it and it has the potential to be done, give no one the right to make you believe it can't be done. You are smart enough to accomplish any goal. With focus and creativity, your contribution and improvement of society is just one thought away. There are no limits to what you can do—just obstacles. Any obstacle can be overcome, conquered, or dominated. It's your choice on how you will get past the obstacles in your life. How far you go is dependent upon what obstacle you stop at. Anything and everything is available to you. As some would say, "The world is yours." Pick where you want to be. Pick what you want to do, and pick how you will spend the rest of your life; it's all available to you.

Anything you haven't done should only be because you haven't done it yet. Don't avoid the life that you are attracted to. If it could be a worthy accomplishment, then give it your all. Your new life can start with a book you read or a topic you study. I've had many pivotal moments in my life because of an article that I read that changed my life forever. As you read, you'll discover that there are more options available to you. The more you study or research things that interest you, the more you realize how

> *If you decide to do it and it has the potential to be done, give no one the right to make you believe it can't be done.*

you can take steps toward where you want to be. Your new life can start with a conversation. By hearing the experience of someone else, it may compel you to experience more of a life. You are restricted only by your imagination. By filling your imagination with the new information and fresh ideas, you'll release yourself from any psychological restrictions. The biggest and best days of your life are awaiting your anticipated arrival. No matter your personal experiences, available capital, or connections (or lack thereof), anything is possible for you.

VALUE OTHERS

The best way to love life is to love people. People are drawn to one another and cannot help but to communicate on some level even if they're strangers. Having good relationships is all part of living a productive life. Maintain your relational optimism as you will meet many people in your life. Keep an ear and eye open for the people you'll meet that you won't be able to live without. There are great people in your future who you will make an impactful difference on and vice versa. Human interaction is one of the pleasures of life that should be enjoyed frequently. Appreciating the value of people and their uniqueness creates gratitude within you. There are many stories of great people that will add fuel to your inner fire as you pursue your dreams. A person's growth or lack thereof can help you evaluate where you are as a human being.

If you expect to build healthy relationships, the well-being of others must be important to you. Everyone serves some level of importance even if you never meet her. What will make you one of the best people on this planet is that you desire the best for other people. Desiring that other people accomplish their dreams should motivate you as you accomplish yours. Make impactful decisions with your life so that your success possesses substance.

People are naturally interactive. We are designed that way to help each other and make each other stronger. It is the unique quality of people that will make you appreciate the beauty that is created when you are connected to the right people.

DON'T KILL YOUR WORTH

Your value increases when you become a reputable person. Don't do whatever causes your reputation to be tarnished and your integrity to be put into question. Style and charisma alone will not make you preferred by people. Your worth is predicated upon you being trusted with much. Your ability to make a promise and over-deliver creates your image. This is the image that people will see before they see your natural face.

Live by the words you speak.

Weigh your words carefully because it's easy to say anything. Without hesitation, step up to every challenge that is thrown your way. The more challenges you can handle, the further you will go.

> *The more challenges you can handle, the further you will go.*

Never stop learning so that in your honesty, you acquire information that gives you different routes to take. Those that will dedicate their lives to honorable practices will always be positioned for optimal benefit. Honesty and transparency should be your two best friends. They will protect you when all else fails. Their ways and concepts have been around for thousands of years and have stood the test of time. Lying requires constant backtracking and keeping up with the lies that were made. Honesty allows for a peaceable life. An honest lifestyle is nothing like the tormented lifestyle of a liar who is doomed to failure.

A transparent person is not afraid to leave him or herself vulnerable to exposure because if exposure ever occurred, the findings would be respectable. Putting integrity before prosperity increases the longevity of their prosperity. You will value yourself better than anyone, so it's best to maintain a high bar for your integrity and raise that bar as you go forward. Set your standards high so that your goals will always be lofty and your vision will always be fresh.

BE NATURALLY PERSUASIVE, NOT MANIPULATIVE

If you believe in what you're doing, others will too. There's nothing like a motivated person attempting to motivate others about the same thing. The choice of words and the ability to communicate will all be enhanced when she speaks of something they believe in. Doing something that you believe in is the best way to convince others of the significance of what you're doing. In life, others will want to know if what you're doing is important and why it is worth their attention. It's not that difficult to convince others of the importance of what you're doing when your heart is involved. The more something means to you, the easier it is for others to get the picture.

Entire lives are spent developing strategies and techniques on how to sway people in the direction you want them to go. Often people's manipulative tactics are exposed for what they really are, which is cheap tactics that only work on the naïve and foolish. Scammers and their scams are never appreciated, just tossed into the ever-growing history file of scams. Without the extra fluff, you can just be authentic and original. Genuine drive and tenacity are always captivating. Who doesn't like a motivated person who is intelligent as well? It's better that your character maintains your name for you by being undoubtedly authentic.

You don't have to do tricks or be a magician to get ahead. Cheating should always be out of the question, and your best effort should always be given. Your integrity will be challenged and your consistency will be put to the test. Anyone can be anything when there's no resistance. True self-development occurs when you attempt to be who you are, against the odds. Boldness and confidence are strengthened the most when weakness is avoided even when it becomes the easy route to take.

Chapter 9:
Lead Yourself First

YOUR PURPOSE AND DESTINY AND goals in life are not the responsibilities of anyone else. You can't wait for somebody to lead you toward the right direction or believe that all the right answers for your life can be found in somebody else. You must first lead yourself.

Wake yourself up early in the morning. Go to bed at the right time. Set goals and accomplish them. Do whatever it is that you set out to do before you even make the attempt to lead someone else. What makes a good leader is someone who can lead his own self. The world is full of people who love leadership positions and have no idea on how to lead. A good leader knows how to encourage and inspire someone to do great things. Even more so, a great leader knows how to give unbiased advice that will help someone find the best direction for their own life. Good leaders pull at the leadership inside of potential would-be leaders in such a way that their lives begin to change.

Have you ever made the attempt to see the greatness in someone else? Try seeing the good in someone else, and focus on it. Develop the good qualities of someone else. Develop a positive outlook in someone else; that's what makes a great leader, not just telling someone what to do. Whatever direction you have succeeded in leading yourself, that's exactly what you use to lead other people. It is taught by some that to be a good leader all you need to do is be a good talker; good talk has never resulted in building wealth or doing anything of significance.

How to Lead Yourself

It is a belief that if you just get the right people around you, you'll be okay. That is only half the battle, as you have to make decisions for yourself. People can influence you to take action, but they can't take action for you. Only you can do for yourself. So with the decisions you made for yourself, what have been the results? If the results have been good, then I think it's more than likely you are going to lead people well. If the results have not been so good, then you can expect to lead people where you have led yourself. It is not possible to do horribly when it comes to leading yourself and at the same time do well when it comes to directing others. If you let things slide with yourself, then you'll let them slide with other people. If you're not self-disciplined, then you can expect to lead others into unproductive habits.

What do your habits look like? Do you keep pushing forward only when you feel like it, or have you developed a healthy and consistent pattern? When you're leading others, you won't be perfect; however, you should work toward perfection. Whatever your personal philosophy is, is the philosophy those that follow you will adapt to. The goal as a leader is to make the leaders in other people come out. Too many leaders seek only to tell others what to do and therefore produce nothing but humans with robotic thinking. When a leader has experience in leading himself or herself, they become more empathetic and well-rounded as it relates to dealing with others' emotions, attitudes, and beliefs. A good leader knows how to analyze and identify with people quickly because she had to deal with herself often.

Would You Follow Yourself?

We all have had encounters with horrible bosses than whom we feel we can do a much better job. So ask yourself, would you be the type that people regret following after, or would they be willing participants in the things you do? Without being biased, consider the things that you dislike in others. It could be dishonesty, lack of motivation, or arrogance. Are the things that you dislike in others part of your character? This is usually a surprise for many when they discover they had become the type of person they don't like. It's nothing to be ashamed of, it is something to work on. Become the type of person that you would respect and admire. Some years ago, I made a list of attributes of the type of person I wanted to be and all the characteristics that would make this person. This list gave me a guideline to work toward in order to become the person I wanted to be. Each day, I am getting closer to becoming the person I want to be, and it all started by simply identifying what areas I needed to work on. Everything about you can change so long as you want them to.

WHEN YOU GROW, SO WILL OTHERS

As a perpetually developing leader, your philosophies, knowledge, and outlooks affect everything and everyone that is connected to you. Everything about you will be reflected in your possessions and relationships. You are the rock that causes a ripple effect. In many ways, whatever trends you start will be the trend of what is connected to you. With that understanding comes great excitement and responsibility. You'll become more aware of what you do because you'll see the fruits of it in what's connected to you. As children resemble their parents even if they don't spend a lot of time with them, so will everything in your life resemble you. If you plan to achieve any goal, you can never have enough accountability. Your life will evidence whether or not you're growing. You must be able to take accountability for whatever your life has produced, good or bad.

PART FOUR:
WALK AWAY

CHAPTER 10:
MOST PEOPLE LOSE

MOST PEOPLE HAVE THE SAME thought patterns and have the same ways of thinking and have the same ways of living; in other words, most people's lives are going to begin and end in the same way. In one of his speeches, one of my all-time favorite speakers, Jim Rohn, made the statement "Walk away." He went on to instruct the audience to walk away from the 97 percent. Don't do what they do. Don't say what they say or talk the way they talk. He was referring to the large number of people that do the same things and live the same lives and wonder why their lives resemble others' failures. Jim Rohn was on to something. As I dug a little deeper, I found that over 80 percent of people who dream to write a book never do. Over 90 percent of U.S. citizens will retire broke. Over 90 percent of U.S. citizens are the least wealthy of our country. Over 80 percent of college graduates will pursue careers that have nothing to do with their college education. Over a third of U.S. citizens are obese. Over 90 percent of Americans' wealth is controlled by 1 percent of Americans. Over 70 percent of all stock investors are speculators, and only 30 percent are actually investing. Over 20 percent of all salespeople, businesses in any industry, and professionals, make 80 percent of all the money in their fields.

These numbers simply show that it is not wise to take the popular route to success, which is to do what most people are doing.

Walk away!!! Don't do what everybody else does.

Most people hate their jobs. Over 10 percent of Americans control U.S. wealth. Over 90 percent of American people cannot retire from the income of their own resources. Most Americans do the same thing, think the same way, and act the same way in finances, health, careers, and relationships. It is your assignment to walk away from what everybody else does and join the few. Musicians, movie stars, athletes, and corporate shares are owned by 10 percent of the people. I hope it is starting to click for you. Most people do the same failing things. Here's what I say to you: "Walk away!" Don't wait until your family or friends agree with your newfound change of heart; walk away as quickly as possible. Walk away from the status quo. Walk away from the norm. Walk away from plans and ideas that don't work. Change directions quickly.

Change the way that you speak. Most people just talk about the most recent events and about what other people are up to. Or they'll just go on and on about things that are not important. A great mind tends to discuss ideas, possibilities, how to serve, and how to make something better. They speak in a sense of innovation, not gossip. Change your eating habits; most people eat out or are fast-food junkies (hint: the reason most people are obese). Change your eating habits, and you'll probably live the life that you're supposed to live. Live in the time that was allotted to you, don't die internally because of neglect.

If you want to win at anything, you have to do what the masses don't. Following the masses may not destroy you, it will prevent you from reaching your desired goals. Not doing what the masses do may include not doing what some of your family and friends do.

> *It is not intelligent to go to someone simply because you know them, but seek out the best people in whatever it is that you want to achieve.*

It is your immediate circle of friends and family that will influence you the most. I am not telling you to constantly isolate yourself; however, you will find it very necessary to periodically isolate yourself for the sake of evaluating your habits. For everything you want to do it, would be wise for you to seek the best in that particular area. If you want to continue growing your business, then surround yourself with the best business talent. If you want to be a better father, then seek out parents who have raised successful children to find out parenting ideas. It is not intelligent to go to someone simply because you know them, but seek out the best people in whatever it is that you want to achieve.

THE STRENGTH TO WALK AWAY

To walk away from what you have adapted to takes strength. I believe that the "finding" of the strength to do so is the reason most people stay where they are. There are so many reasons we can give ourselves to fail or quit. The truth is that no one has to stay in an unwanted condition.

Most people have the strength to walk away but don't use it.

Conditioning yourself to embrace your weakness takes no strength. There are better circumstances you can position yourself to encounter when you walk away from unhealthy situations. You do have the strength to walk away from anything you don't want to be a part of. At this moment, you must realize that you should not work for what is working against you. It's not in anyone's best interest to work at a job that consistently takes advantage of him. If you would not work for a job that takes advantage of you, then don't work for habits or relationships that work against you. Come out of an impotent condition so that you can see that life is still going on for you. Move fearlessly away from people and things that keep you weak and distracted. Don't allow being in the wrong atmospheres to smother you as a sheet covers a dead body. If there is air in your body, then there is still much for you to accomplish. If you still have thoughts of becoming better, that is a sign your body has enough strength to take the right steps. Don't look for the strength you already have to be discovered in other people. Your strength will not be confirmed in somebody else. Don't continue another day in life believing that your condition is the result of someone not helping you, when the real problem is having an attitude that expects others to do the work for them. You can go a lot further in life if you will not wait for people to give you strength. No one will give you your strength. Even when a person inspires you, they are inspiring what is already inside of you. You have more than enough strength to make right-now decisions. With your strength, take right-now actions.

THE REASON TO WALK AWAY

Crowds are filled with lots of people. What is common about crowds is that they tend to attract even more people, hence the reason lots of people have failing businesses, lots of people have failing marriages, lots of people lose money in the stock exchange and lots of people lose their health due to bad decisions or negligence. What is very consistent about these things is that lots of people do them. Having the same actions as lots of people, is the result of being attracted to a crowd. In grade school, I was always told to stay away from the crowd. Now also in my adult life, staying away from the crowd has actually worked to my advantage. Crowds are usually filled with people following each other's actions. What has benefited my life tremendously is detaching myself from the crowd, so that I am not a product of the crowd. It is not intelligent to believe that you would get a different result by sticking with these largely numbered crowds. These numbers are so large because it is always easier to follow the popular trend. Doing what everyone else does will ultimately get you the results of everyone else.

There are people that I consider professionals at looking one way and acting in an entirely different way. Pretending to have success is no one's hope for their life. Instead of looking well, actually become well. If you are ever at a loss on what to do, the crowd will always show you exactly what not to do.

The people you are connected to do play a major role in your life. What you are around and who you are around tend to affect the path you take. It becomes obvious in what direction you're going in based on the company you keep. It is widely taught that you don't burn bridges for the sake of maintaining relationships. In some cases, burning bridges may be your only hope to the success you want. If the bridges you have only connect you to the opposite of what you want, then let them burn. Choose to walk away from the things and people you've outgrown. Your progress cannot be hindered by convenience. It is never smart to stick to what you know doesn't work. Remember, the perfect time to make good decisions will probably never come, so it should be done now.

SHOULDN'T I KEEP WHAT I GOT TO GET WHAT I WANT?

For years one of my closest relatives would always tell me, "Keep what you got to get what you want." I have found this to be advice that will set you back in every area of life, if what you have are bad things. Actually, most people could never get what they want because what they already have is standing in their way. People want greater success, though they have a philosophy that is contrary to what they want. If you still believe that riches are just for rich people, you probably won't get there. Riches are available to all of us who are willing to learn the simple principles to acquire it. If what you have is the wrong thing, you'll never get the right thing. Be willing to let all the wrong things go and burn the bridges that are keeping you from where you want to be. Never hold on to what you have if what you have is worthless anyway. If necessary, move what you have out of the way to get what you want.

When Do I Start the Process?

There is never the perfect time to do anything. If you can take steps in the right direction, do it now. Never wait for the perfect position to come before you take the perfect action, because the perfect position or the perfect action to take may never come. The best time to make significant changes to your life is always now—better yet, right now. When you change you are literally walking towards your new life and walking away from your old life. Anyone that has held you back, classify him as old. More than just the people around you, you yourself may be the person you may have to walk away from. You'll never actually walk outside of your skin and leave yourself behind. I'm actually referring to the old you, the old ways, the old philosophies, and the old habits you should run away from if they have not brought you the success you desire.

Run toward a Better Life

There is a small amount of people who have successful marriages, businesses, and good health. That's exactly what you're walking toward—the few people who've decided not to be another statistic and the mavericks that represent the small amount of people who decided to walk away from the crowds. Walk toward the greatest life you can imagine for yourself. My friend Ed Keels likes to put it this way: Don't get stuck on the island, "Some-day-I'll". A person who lives on this island speaks the "Some-day-I'll" language. It sounds like this: Some-day-I'll start a business. Some-day-I'll get in shape. Some-day-I'll change my views, and the list goes on and on. No one seems to ever remember being on the island, yet they speak the language very well.

Chapter 11:
Change the Status Quo

A N ORIGINAL ALWAYS PROSPERS. LET me make myself clear: change the status quo, not reinvent the wheel. Change what is normally expected of someone in your field, industry or profession. Be brave enough to be innovative, intuitive, and different. What will really makes you a true individual is saying what has never been said before and doing what has never been done before. If you have nothing else to say but what's already been said, and you do what already has been done, you will classify yourself as the norm. The best way to be different is simply to be you. You are naturally different. You are naturally unique. You are naturally special. You don't have to spend your time becoming a wannabe, an I-should-be, a look-a-like, or a something-like. Who needs a copycat? From this point on, all you need to do is take your natural uniqueness, your natural distinction, and package it up to be presented it to the world. Your intentions should be to contribute to the world what you were naturally supposed to. Make your contribution to the world now, so that this world will have to change. Imagine this world experiencing a uniqueness that it never experienced because it could only come through you. You have a chance to make this world better than the way you found it the day you were born. Be Different!

You Never Live Until You Live

Living life is better when you're living your life and not someone else's. Never wait for life to be lived for you. Danger, excitement, thrill, fear of doing your best at something, embarrassment, and success should all be embraced because they're all part of life. You can live a rich and fulfilling life, or you can waste away and die. It's your choice.

Remember this, Shadows Are Dark. Let the light hit your face, and come out of the darkness of being in someone else's shadows. To learn from someone is one thing, to live your life—your entire life—after them is another. The development that comes from being a protégé is temporal, not permanent. If you allow yourself to be behind someone else permanently, you'll begin to cripple yourself and put yourself in a position to be limited. Even as you lead others, you may need some guidance for yourself from time to time, that doesn't require you to come under somebody. Never limit yourself because of the fear of not being good enough. If you meditate on your shortcomings, you will never be good enough, tall enough, good-looking enough, pretty enough, or slim enough. Remember, you will always be just enough to be a great version of you.

Don't live in other people's shadows.

MAKE THE WORLD BETTER

I bet with what you've seen and heard thus far in your life, you have a lot of innovative ideas that can benefit many ways of life. You are capable of doing good things in this life. Even though for years you have heard many other names as being great, remember, your name is good enough.

Make your name great. Don't just hope to be famous, hope to be great. Become a respectable and honorable person by doing your best in all that you do. Believe it or not, your name will be as great as you allow it to be. Many of us are used to hearing other people's names be given recognition, maybe now it's time for you to make your mark. Never spend your days trying to be the next professional imitator. You have a better chance at becoming the first you. It is a dream for many to be mentioned amongst great names. Have a better dream, by becoming a great name to be mentioned amongst. In whatever you decide to do, remember your name is good enough. Now, since you know that, let others find out. Let your name be the name that challenges the status quo. Let your name be the name

> *Never spend your days trying to be the next professional imitator.*

that spearheads a new industry or new era of industry. Make your name into what it's supposed to be, not into what everyone says it should be.

Being Unique Is Easy

Being you is the most natural thing you'll encounter. Being yourself is thought of as something difficult to achieve. It only presents difficulty when being yourself is contrary to those around you. Being different will always present some conflict. The status quo is to just hop on board whatever bandwagon is popular at the time. When a person goes against a popular trend or public opinion, then immediately they will stick out like a sore thumb. To stand out that much is exactly what you want. No one wants to be known as the guy who did the same as the other guy. You want to be known for being you. It is your uniqueness that you will always bring to the table. When I speak of your uniqueness, I don't mean your obnoxiousness or being violently confrontational. Who you are from the crown of your head to the soles of your feet creates a separation from you and others without your help. The sound of your voice and the body gestures that only you make will all become your calling card. Your only job is to be you. Put emphasis on the word *be*. Just *be* you. Being something takes action. Being you will take natural action. Without thought or consideration of living in the shadow of someone else, just be you. To be you doesn't take studying millions of books. You will probably pick up personality traits from other people, there will still be no one quite like you. Never be ashamed of the qualities that make you unique. Your hair, your height, your build, and even the things that you like will all make up the all-important you. To stand out won't be so hard either. It comes with being you. Even being misunderstood is a sign of your difference. Being different is not bad; it just may take time for it to be embraced. Our society moves forward from the effects of those that are not of like kind. It is those that are not of like kind that will bring the rest of the world to where they are. Your difference and uniqueness are just what the world needs.

Being an imitator takes way too much unnecessary effort. It takes strength to be you. It will take even more strength to be someone else. You can give yourself more energy to use in a day when you no longer spend it on pretending. You are not made to be someone else. Your biological makeup demands that you be you without interruption. Failure is inevitable when attempting to live out someone else's life. Be confident enough to speak your own tone and walk your own path. Don't spend another day by working diligently to live in the personality of someone else. You have much to offer if you'll be brave enough to offer it. The world may know of other possibilities because you possess them.

CHAPTER 12:
THINK INDEPENDENTLY

N O MATTER HOW MUCH ADVICE, counsel or how much of someone else's experience people share with you, at the end of the day, you will have to make decisions for yourself. What that means is you're going to have to have your own information to make great decisions. Studying, analyzing, and brainstorming are all things that are necessary so that you may develop your opinions. All of your views cannot be based on the views of someone else. Your own views will be the creative fuel to the decisions you make. It is your views that will give you something to approach others with. Whether it be through collaboration or partnering with others, you will have something to bring to the table.

If you let others make decisions for you, then you put your life in the hands of others. Between all the advice and counsel you'll receive, the "do this," and the "do that" lies an unbiased truth. To make a great decision, you need a great source of information; you cannot just depend on what other people tell you. You must be able to take bits and pieces of what you heard, saw, and experienced to put together one great idea for one great conclusion. You'll be surprised as to what comes out of you when you stretch your mind. Critical thinking is for those who want the best results out of their lives; however, many people fail to take the necessary steps to be sure that the decision that they're making is well-thought-out, educated, and not being made out of haste, anger, or disappointment. I'm all for taking a leap of faith. Taking a step of faith in everything doesn't make sense. A dumb decision should not be justified as a step of faith.

COUNSEL IS STILL NECESSARY

Good advice is still necessary for you to make great decisions. Great decisions are usually accompanied by great insight. It is the reason companies create advisory boards. Still, you must truly read between the lines of all the advice that you receive. In business, you'll probably get the advice from a lot of people. Many times the advice you'll receive will come from that person's own perspective. Accountants are more money-focused and cost-focused, entrepreneurs are very zealous while investors may not be as innovative. When you get these different perspectives on one business decision, then you have an opportunity to make a profound choice.

It will be necessary to qualify the people you receive advice from. I personally don't take marital advice from those who never had a good marriage. Also when I get advice on business, I seek those who are qualified in their respective places. It is unlikely that somebody who hasn't had good experiences in an area that you need advice on could lead you in the right direction. Good advice is priceless, so get lots of it. Even with the good advice you accumulated, don't take the fun away from your brain by not figuring things out for yourself. The necessity for advice is to avoid repeating the same mistakes as others. There's no such thing as a new problem that someone has not already dealt with. Leverage the experience of other people so that your experiences are much more enjoyable.

> *It will be necessary to qualify the people you receive advice from.*

DEVELOP YOUR OWN PHILOSOPHY

We all possess ideas and ways of thinking that we believe work for us. It's what our entire lives are built around. Ask yourself, does your philosophy work for you, or is it time to refine your philosophy for a better life? Your actions will only go as far as your philosophy allows you to. If your way of thinking does not agree with something you are interested in, you won't be able to act upon it.

Everybody wants something that they don't have. Those who will get what they want are those who will adapt the right philosophy to get what they want. Your way of thinking will strategically lead you or mislead you. That's why it is important to adapt an effective philosophy and reevaluate your philosophy often. I witnessed senior citizens who have the same problems and patterns of a teenager. This is possible because both possess similar philosophies. Just because you're older than someone, doesn't mean you're smarter than him. You become smarter by adding things that work to your own personal philosophy. Any area in your life in which you've experienced repeated failure is a sign that you need a refreshed philosophy pertaining to that area in your life. Your entire philosophy or your philosophy in a specific area may need to be redefined. If something works for you, don't change it. If something doesn't work for you, don't be afraid to change it.

The goal in developing your own philosophy is to create a winning system of doing things. You are your own person, and your own way of thinking is vital for your own life. Consider your philosophy toward time management, relationships, business, health, how you raise your children, and education. It's easy never to consider these things, never considering your own heart toward different matters will leave your life to chance. Whether you know it or not, you do possess a personal philosophy. It's better that you take ownership of your philosophy and way of thinking because it will do its job of dictating your actions. Your ideas, your planning, your goals, and your actions will all go back to your philosophy agreeing with them or not. When I wanted to lose weight I discovered that I possessed a destructive philosophy toward exercising, thus maintained a weight problem. Having a destructive philosophy toward anything will equal unwanted results. Destroy your destructive philosophy before it destroys you. There are many good things right behind a winning philosophy. Winning philosophies never just work in one area. The right philosophy will bleed into multiple areas of your life.

The best philosophy to adapt is one that embraces integrity, honesty, and fairness. Believing in the power of having a good character helps in adopting the right philosophy. As time passes, it will be necessary to touch up your philosophy and give yourself an even better chance at life.

NO ONE CAN TELL YOU WHAT TO THINK

Any good investor will tell you that no one can tell you what to do with your money. And the same is true with your life. No one can tell you what to do with your life. It will be from your own knowledge and appraisals that you make your final decisions. You will have the final decision in every area in your life. No one will hold your hand and tell you exactly what to do. Knowing that you will not be babysat should empower you, not scare you. There will be lots of decisions you will have to make, so let those decisions be your own choices and not the choices made through you by other people. You are not the conduit which people live their lives through. You are your own man. You are your own woman. Whatever you decide to do, you will be held responsible for that choice. If you make a bad decision you will have to face the consequences, so it's better that you be rewarded for a good decision that you make.

No one can tell you how to think, when to think, what to think, or how to feel. It will be totally up to you. Even when someone gives you excellent advice, it will be you who decides to use it. Making the best decisions for you starts with having excellent information. Having a one-dimensional mind is a recipe for ignored options and missed opportunities. Be willing to think outside your own room. Thinking independently doesn't mean ignoring the entire world. Thinking independently consists of using information that is available to you to come up with your own analysis. Of course, your own experiences will play a role in your analysis. It is important that those experiences aren't allowed to override what is obvious. Common sense does have its place when optimism distorts your judging abilities. I've dealt with people who showed me that they have zero integrity. If I'm not careful, optimism could cause me to overlook what is right in front of my face. I used basic common sense to decide not to work with them. No optimism was needed.

Good ideas can come from many different places. The best minds have learned to use many different ideas and experiences to assist in their decision-making processes. Using what has worked and knowing what has not worked can help in avoiding repeating others' mistakes. Wait for no one to decide what you will do with yourself. When you make career choices, it will be you who will live in the career. When you make relationship decisions, it is you who will be in a relationship. If you are going to be the one living your life, then you should probably be the one deciding for your life, too.

INDEPENDENCE IS LIBERATING

Give yourself autonomy. There is a high, a thrill, and a drive that you can only get from knowing when your independence is in motion. Independence means, "I depend from within." Never confuse independence with arrogance and stupidity. Even an independent individual understands that qualified counsel becomes necessary sometimes. Every day, strive toward independence. Learn as much as you can to make your own decisions. Gain the ability to know what's necessary for you without hundreds of opinions. Be wise enough to make choices while not depending on others' opinions, thoughts, and ideas. Free your life through independent choices. Make choices that put you in control of your life and in control of your days. Never make anybody your crutch again. Freedom for you is just a few choices away.

GIVE YOURSELF PERMISSION

Say yes to yourself before anybody else says yes to you. You have to know that what you set out to do is going to work before anybody else does. It's one thing to start something; it's another thing to believe it is going to be done. Goal-setting and having the guts to achieve something can be put on hold if you will not permit yourself first.

There are millions of people with opinions who say that they're going to make a difference, and will only gather enough strength to point their fingers at someone else. At the very moment they have an opportunity to do something, they'll just believe it's someone else's responsibility because of an engrafted belief that they're just not fit to do it. If you can give an intelligent opinion about something, you probably know enough to take some sort of action. Committing yourself to do anything frees you from the crushing, "You can't do it" that you'll hear from other people. If you told yourself yes, who could tell you no? Who could deny what you approved? This can sound arrogant, but it is the mentality of a determined person. Failures will give you their failing opinions. Fearful people will give you their fearful opinions. Sometimes a no from someone is rooted in their fear or failure. If you believe it can be done, then who's to say it can't? Life is full of chances for you to do what someone else has never done. If no one has ever done it, then you have a chance to be the first. The first is always remembered. If someone's telling you no about something then it is your right to say yes to yourself.

No one can take your right to believe in yourself. Nor is it possible for someone to steal your dream. Giving yourself permission to excel snatches the authority away from others who don't believe in you. Giving permission means possessing the authority to do so. Who else has authority over you except you? So put to practice permitting yourself to go for your goals. Every day, go for it. Go for what you see inside of your head. Every vision you have should be investigated thoroughly so that action steps are put in place. And with every step you take, remind yourself you can do it because you said so.

> *Say yes to yourself before anybody else says yes to you.*

BE HONEST WITH YOURSELF

If you ever read a business report or a public company's 10-K report, you will find that some executives are pretty honest and some can be pretty alluring. The dishonest executives destroy themselves and the company while the honest ones move the company and themselves forward. Honesty can be pretty embarrassing, either though it will lead you to make the right changes. When you intend to deceive others, you deceive yourself as well. No one wins in the game of dishonesty. If you can start being honest with yourself, then you can actually build trustworthiness with other people. Nowadays, honesty is a rarity, and when you're honest, you put yourself ahead of the pack.

People who stay in the mold of procrastination and stagnation refuse to realize the truth about themselves. It is in the truth that you will find the answer to a problem. If a person can realize that they may move too slowly, then they can figure out how they can speed things up. This can only be done when you're honest with yourself consistently. Telling others the truth is respectable, but telling yourself the truth is even more respectable. Telling yourself the truth puts you in a position to make tough decisions in life because you're not afraid of facing what really is the problem, even if it's you. We have all wished to live in a fantasy land where everything is perfect and right. Nothing's wrong with a fantasy here and there, when you make the attempt to live in that fantasy to escape your reality, you'll only avoid what you eventually will have to deal with. Being an achiever is not running from problems, it's solving them. What will separate you from the herd of wannabe's and those that are achievers is that you can face the facts and come up with a resolution.

How many problems have you avoided due to not being able to face the challenge? It's much easier to lie to yourself to ease the pain of the situation. When history has proven that lying has never results in significant benefits. A big or small lie has always creating more trouble than intended. With the posture of a tree, you must brace yourself for the storm that comes with progress. It is often taught that you should avoid embarrassment at all costs. I've learned to embrace the embarrassing truth if I want to get ahead. Inside of the embarrassing truth lies the answers to a problem you are now free to accept. The embarrassing truth can reveal your flaws, your repeated mistakes, and the errors of your ways. Without confronting the truth about yourself, how would you ever expect to develop? Once you allow yourself to develop, the people and things you're connected to are released to develop as well.

You probably affect more things in your life than you realize. Because of this, there are a lot of things just waiting for you to change. Your household and surroundings will seem to have done a 360-degree turnaround the moment you are honest with yourself. Your best and worst critic will always be you. You are your best critic because no one knows you the way you do, and you are your worst critic because no one knows you like you do. Knowledge of self should not be depressing information, it is simply a chance to realize just who you are and who you're not. When you really know who you are not, you have a better idea of what you need to change to become who you want to be. Whether you are an athlete, professional, stay-at-home mom, college student, be extremely honest with yourself in order to change for the better. The sooner you become honest with yourself, the sooner you begin the process of transformation.

PART FIVE:
BECAUSE YOU CAN

CHAPTER 13:
HIGHER IS BETTER

YOU CAN ABSOLUTELY REACH YOUR fullest potential. Great potential is one of the most undiscovered things amongst people. Great potential will only be discovered when you take action, not just by giving it much thought. How then do you reach your fullest potential? Your greatest potential will be discovered through taking the path that will develop you the most. It is very comfortable to stay where you've been for years. It's very comfortable to do the same things that you normally do on a daily basis; but comfort doesn't develop. Comfort doesn't grow anything.

A muscle can't develop out of comfort. A mind cannot grow in education out of comfort. A body cannot reach its full potential and athleticism if it stays comfortable. Being uncomfortable will make you better. It will make you think hard. Being uncomfortable will always push you to a greater level; henceforth, going higher is better. Have goals that are higher and bigger than you. Having a goal that is higher and bigger than you will push you to extend yourself further than you've ever attempted to. Once you start reaching higher, you instantly put yourself on the path to becoming better. If you spend the rest of your life reaching for things that are already on your level or are already on your playing field, you will never grow as a person. Begin to expand your circle of competence and reach outside of your normal surroundings. Don't subject yourself to getting the same results you've always had by staying in your normal circle of competence; the rest of your life depends on you growing and expanding to new things.

THINK BIG TO GET BIG RESULTS

The power of the mind is evident every day. A negative mind-set can ruin a good opportunity. A broken mind will never be able to grasp new ideas. Our mental perception creates the reality that we live in. Thus, having the wrong mental perception can create a hazardous reality. Rarely do we live in the reality that surrounds us, we mainly in the reality created by our mental perception. Whatever you want, believe, desire, and think inside of your mental perception is what you see outwardly on a day-to-day basis. Your mind can be so focused on your goals that current circumstances cease to exist. You can actually create a world of your own. In your own world, you could have as little or as much as you want. If you want small, think small; if you want big, think extremely big.

Don't get caught thinking small. Thinking small will lead to you only achieving a percentage of your potential. Thinking small puts obstacles in your way that haven't even come yet. During the time that I was homeless, I was seeking multiple ways to create an income. Little did I know, the answer to my question was to think about how I could be of some benefit to someone else's life or institution in a big way. After talking to a mortgage originator about acquiring foreclosed properties, I was able to acquire six debt-free properties for a nonprofit group before I ever got my own place. Thinking bigger than your own situation places you in a position to transcend into better situations. Thinking big knows no limitations. Every day you have a chance to affect someone in a positive way with your touch, talent, and/or abilities.

WHO KNOWS WHAT YOU CAN DO?

There really is no limit to what you can do. No one, not even yourself, really knows all of what you are capable of. Once you accomplish one thing, you'll seek to do another thing, and another, and eventually, you'll be doing things that you never even imagined yourself doing. Your life is not fully made up of just your past. Your life is also made up of the possibilities of your future. Many will try to predict your future, and no one is definitely sure, one thing you can be certain about is that you will give every day your all. Your talents and capabilities have so much room to grow no matter how developed they are. As you accomplish parts of your vision, your vision will become bigger because your life is meant to grow perpetually. Stay healthy and motivated so that your best days remain in front of you. Nothing is more depressing than to live in your past. Even if your past was great, your future can be greater. As you continue to learn and educate yourself, there's no telling the level of intellect you will operate on.

Spend the rest of your life discovering all your potential. You only become too spread out when you're doing a lot of things you really have no interest in. When you do what you're interested in, it really isn't work. When you have a great interest in something, you can learn all there is to know about it, without caring about the workload that is involved. That's the power of having a great interest in something. There's no telling what you can do if you stay enthusiastic and optimistic about life. The only limits you have are the ones you set for yourself. Your impact on politics, business, or your local neighborhood are all possible if you believe so. As your body recharges during your night sleep, it allows your vigor and tenacity to get a good charge as well.

This is not your time to quit. When it's your time to take a rest, it won't be to quit, it will be to get ready for the next best chapter of your life. Life does get better as it goes on. It can be difficult to take steps forward, but the resistance will only build your strength. Things that used to be hard won't be so difficult after you've gone through them. So get through everything that you face, and live to tell the story with a smile. My advice to you is to find out all the good about yourself that you have not discovered yet. Your time is coming—just be sure that you're ready. Just be sure that every day you hold nothing back.

BECAUSE YOU CAN

Because you can do something good, you should do it. To be any less is disgraceful. Allow your good ideas to flow. Be good at your profession. Do the best you can everywhere you can. You'll never really need a good excuse to do a good deed. You can do good simply because the opportunity presented itself or because of our human nature to help when we can. This means more than being a good citizen, it means inspiring others through your good works. People do watch other people, so give them something good to look at. Everything good about you should be shown to the world. Doing good, becoming great, and affecting people's lives are necessities, not privileges. It's within all of us to do extraordinary things that make the world we live in a lot better. Let your good works become second nature to you.

You Don't Need (Others') Permission to Succeed

It doesn't matter if someone says you can or can't do something. It doesn't matter if someone says you're too tall, too short, too big, or too small. It doesn't matter what anyone says about you. What does matter is what you say about yourself. Whatever you say about yourself will always be true even if it hasn't happened yet. What you believe about yourself is the most important thing to consider. A complement doesn't even have an effect on you unless you believe it. By over-considering what someone says about you, you give them permission over you. Your confidence or success should never be contingent upon the yes or no of someone else. Even rejection should have its limits in your life. Only you can permit what you will and will not do. Where you will and will not go should always be in your hands. Children need permission from their parents because their parents are the authorities in their lives. As an adult, you represent the authority in your life. Thus, permission must come from you. When you permit yourself to go further in life, you take that permission away from others who may not agree. You are not an animal on a leash, waiting to be tugged in the right direction. If someone has authority in your life, let it be because you gave it to him or her and not because it was taken.

Your voice means more to you than anyone else's voice. You can talk yourself into something, and you can talk yourself out of it. Waiting for someone to give you permission to make your own decisions puts you at a huge disadvantage. Why give up your authority? Others who won't permit you to move forward are probably afraid that you'll move ahead of them. Don't let the fear of someone else stop you. You have every right to permit yourself to succeed. Living on the permission of others is beneath you. Let go of negative ideas and philosophies of other people. You owe it to yourself.

How Far Will You Reach?

When a person exercises and they feel a slight burn in their muscles, it is their muscles stretching beyond their normal comfort. When your muscles stretch beyond their normal comfort, that is when they begin to grow and develop. Your life reflects the same process. Only when you stretch beyond your normal comfort, and only then, will you grow. When critical moments come that force you to think beyond your normal parameters, that is when you find new ideas. Everything in your life grows the moment it is stretched. Being stretched physically and mentally can bring out the best or worst version of you. It could bring out your best when you endure what feels like too much for you. It could bring out your worst when you refuse to reach past where you are.

I knew of an elderly man who suffered from physical body pains for years. Medicine or doctor visits seemed to not work for him at all. It wasn't until he attended a martial arts class that his health started to improve. What made the difference was that he needed to be mobile. He needed to be working his body to improve its overall health, not sitting on a couch and being dependent upon a drug prescribed by a doctor to make a difference. Sitting and hoping will not make any changes in your life. Pushing and driving yourself to go further and further each day will align you with a better life. You won't see where you really could be until you do whatever it takes to get there. Learning, taking action, and even failing will play a role in your overall growth. It would be obvious to think that if you stay at home, never take a risk, and stay in your place, then life would be easy. Playing it safe only diminishes your strength and mental health. The mind, body, and soul all need a push that only comes from living life to its fullest.

When you stretch yourself, you allow yourself the opportunity to enjoy what life has to offer you. Having great vision and never taking action is the equivalent of a delusional person seeing a mirage. Oh, how horrible it is to desire something and not even be able to touch it. That's too close to self-torture. Be willing to be stretched by confronting every challenge, knowing that your goal is to see the challenge through to reach your peak potential.

Everything Is within Your Reach

Anything and everything will seem far away if you never reach for them. As you stretch in your knowledge, character, and strength, you'll see that everything you want is within your reach. Don't consider anything impossible if you haven't reached for it yet. I love when I come up with new ideas. I hated when I shared those ideas with people who refused to consider the possibility of accomplishing something that they never did. *Consider yourself able to accomplish anything you will seriously consider.* There's really nothing on this earth that you can't learn with a little diligence. Whoever you need to connect with to accomplish your goal is not that far away. Everything in life is actually closer than you think. When I say everything in life is closer than you think, I don't mean it will fall on your lap. What I do mean is that what you think may take a decade to accomplish will probably take a lot less time. What you think you can't do, you probably can do better than others. Whatever's standing in your way is something you're probably stronger than.

It's all a matter of taking a chance on yourself. Reaching beyond your limits will always have its benefits. I've met a lot of people in a very short amount of time, and what separates those who are achievers and those who are not are very simple differences. On one end of the spectrum, people live in fear and are very content. On the other end of the spectrum, the achievers never stop learning, planning, and reaching for their best. Much of the world would rather not try to succeed and blame their conditions on other people without realizing that there's really nothing standing in their way but themselves.

Refuse to adapt to mediocrity. Adapt to good things only and not what people and conditions force you to adapt to. It will always be easier to lie down and die. There's even a temptation to keep your potential lying dormant inside of you. There will be many urges and reasons given to you to be less of yourself. It will be your job to put these urges and temptations in their place—that place being out of your life. There are too many challenges for you to conquer to get stuck at one challenge. Never allow the option to settle for less to become your option. Go as high as you want in life without anyone's permission. Let your success be your choice, and don't wait for someone else to decide how far you'll go. With great intensity, intentionally reach for what you want. Every time you reach, you'll discover that you can do more than what you did before.

If you want better relationships, it's all in how far you're willing to reach for it by doing something you've never done before in a relationship. If you want more respect, reach for it by demanding respect through making respectable decisions. You can have anything if you'll reach far and long enough for it.

LIFE WILL CONTINUE EVEN IF YOU WAIT

Procrastinators and wanderers never seem to realize that life is passing them by while they continually reconsider the same decisions. While others worry about what can go wrong, there's another group taking the initiative and finding out what can go right. The longer you wait in life, the more things pass you by. No matter what, time will move on. People will move on. You should move on as well. Waiting too long can be just the same as not doing anything. Some like to call their years of not doing anything a long wait. Giving something a different name doesn't change what it is. Either you're moving forward or you're moving backward.

Doing too much of a bad thing is really bad. Waiting, guessing, and staying uncertain can place you in the worst days of your life. Anybody can come up with hundreds of excuses as to why they are not where they want to be. As my friend John Wood would say, "Excuses are nothing more than justified lies." These justified lies are used to blindfold yourself from your undiscovered potential. Remember, while you make excuses, someone's making an effort and excusing their reasons to quit out the window. You can choose your life, or a life can choose you. You can choose to be what you want to be, or what you don't want to be will choose you. Don't let another day of your life perish because of neglect. How many opportunities do you allow to pass you by because you were nonchalant? Snap out of your worst days, and enter into your best days. Put your old habits behind you, and never let what could be your best moments pass you by. Pay attention to the good in your life as that will help you avoid stagnation. Each of your days deserves your best attention, your best ideas, and your best attitudes. Without giving the day what it deserves, you can't what you want out of the day.

Don't hope for another thing that you won't go after. Deferring your dreams will spoil your appetite for life. You won't be able to do everything, but what you can do, do them well. Life is moving forward; are you moving with it? To be progressive, you must be innovative. Never stop creating, believing, hoping, and taking steps in the right direction.

You're Thinking Too Small

Small thinking benefits no one. Small thinkers can only see their current situations without considering the multitude of possibilities that lie ahead. Small thinking is sickening and has no place for those who want more out of life. Even if you start small, always think BIG. The world will never be affected by what you do if you think small. Thinking big means considering the millions of people you can inspire instead of just inspiring yourself. Thinking big makes a tough situation easier to deal with. Thinking big has its benefits for many and not just one. Small minds speak in the sense of "maybe it will happen." Big minds speak in the sense of "it will happen."

You can never think big enough or learn enough. Life becomes fun when you begin to actively pursue big ideas. Make your goals bigger and your dreams larger. Don't be afraid of the possibility of failure. Failures are nothing more than mishaps that could be used to your advantage. The challenges of accomplishing big things are what make them fun and interesting. Enlarging your thinking will help others obtain a greater vision as well. When people see you pursuing your goals, it will inspire them to do the same. Just as pessimism is contagious, so is optimism and enthusiasm. Keeping a smile on your face and an enthusiastic attitude create life wherever you go. Just your attitude alone can change many people.

CHAPTER 14:
FEAR AND DOORS

B EHIND YOUR GREATEST FEAR IS life—your life. Doors and fears are the same thing. Let me plead my case: a door will get you from one side to the other (hint: a fear will get you from one side to the other as long as you go through it). Before you go through a door, you first have to turn the knob and push; the same thing with fear. Before you go through fear, you have to connect to it and move it out of the way, and then you will be exposed on what's on the other side. Fear is something that you can't run from because it will show up whenever there are big situations or whenever there is a tough decision. Fear is only in your life so you can conquer it. Let's be clear: some doors are harder to open than others. Some doors are heavy. Some doors are rusted shut. Some doors have security systems on them. All in all, it just takes approaching a door and going through it by any means necessary. Some doors need to be kicked down. Some doors need to be knocked down. Some doors are totally going to take a sledgehammer; it doesn't matter what it takes as long as you go through. Some doors lead you to an area, and that's the only door, so if you are afraid of life, it may be because it's the only way to get to your destination. You shouldn't wait around because you leave the destination waiting longer, but by standing the test of getting to your door, you'll find yourself in a new place in life.

WHAT IS FEAR?

Fear is the idea that something bad could happen. Which is completely natural because our creative abilities allow us to imagine good as well as bad. As long as your mind and imagination stay healthy, you will occasionally consider fearful thoughts. It is an absolute must to be able to foresee good and bad consequences. When we foresee bad, it can sometimes create fear in our emotion. Fear is only conquered when you go against the emotions that embrace fear. Fear can cause people to do many things, especially going into hiding and stay there. The best way to conquer that is to come out of hiding and never go back. Doing the complete opposite of what fear commissions you to do keeps the conqueror alive inside of you.

CONQUER MORE

Those that are satisfied in life will stay content, while the rest of us will always look for the next thing to conquer. The same is true in any profession. You can learn something and begin to plateau. To continually grow you must stay hungry to dominate your own limitations. At whatever level you're on, there is always more for you to accomplish. Think above and beyond accomplishing more for yourself and seriously consider the impact you can have through your achievements. What you do in life gives others the awakening and inspiration to achieve their goals. You are the conduit between people and what life could be if they take a chance. Take it as your personal responsibility to inspire someone else, for humans have always inspired other humans. Look for what you can do next in this life. You're not short of ideas or talents. Your best has yet to be witnessed by others or yourself. Someone needs you to succeed so they'll know that they can do the same. Someone needs you to teach her what you've learned. You're not becoming better every day just for you, it is also for the greater contribution you will make to others people's lives.

Refuse to be afraid of becoming better. Fear should never be an indicator to quit, it should always be an indicator that you are on the right track. Only give fear what it deserves—a slap in the face. Every time you go past the limitation of fear, you turn fear into a platform for your own glory. Let fear motivate you, not distract you. Let fear compel you, not limit you. Confront fear and never let it restrain you. Beat fear at one level to beat fear at another level.

THE COMPLICATION OF FEAR

It is common to have knowledge that you can do something while not being sure how you're going to get there. You could have butterflies in your stomach when you think about the things you want to do, and at a moment's notice feel entirely different about the same things. Fear can complicate the ideas of accomplishing your goals. You can know that something is within your reach, but it feels so far away. To have such a strong desire and to have that desire challenged on a daily basis can make you feel defeated. Fear likes to show up when you're right at point of you separating yourself from your past and coming into your future. You'll be attracted to something and afraid of it at the same time. These are things we all have to face, but we all have the opportunity move forward and not be stuck in the place of complex emotions. Never get stuck at the complexity of fear. One of the most exciting experiences in life is being afraid to do a thing and overcoming it. It is one of the true pleasures of life—to desire something and finally obtain it.

Complications, complexity, excitement, pain, and other similar symptoms occur when a woman is pregnant. And after all of her suffering, the end result is a beautiful baby. Give your baby, your dreams, and your destiny a chance to be born by seeing the pregnancy all the way through. Endure the emotions—the fights, the fears, and the challenges—to get a greater result.

When faced with opportunity, you can feel as if you're in a tug-of-war. Should I or shouldn't I? "What is this?" and "What is that?" can be the most obvious questions you would ask yourself. You quickly realize that part of being excited is also a mixture of certainty and nervousness. Simply get out of your own way. Don't put your right foot in front of your left foot to trip yourself. Don't become your own brick wall.

BE CONTRARY TO FEAR

Doing the opposite of fear should be put into practice every day. Considering what could go wrong, the embarrassment if everything doesn't go right, and the potential losses of a failed endeavor (plus emotions) equals a lot of fear. Fear creates a reality where nothing goes the way it's supposed to. Fear also imposes on its victims during the most important times of their lives. When fear is embraced, it has a voice that will sound just like your own. Just as most children habitually rebel against their parents, the same attitude must be developed toward fear. With a smile on your face, do exactly the opposite of what fear tells you to do.

Fear happens when you have a high skepticism of what could possibly go wrong. Before you even take the first step toward something, fear would say, "Don't take that step." Your journey will only begin with your first step that is taken. And that step will have to come out of rebellion to fear. You can still be afraid and move forward. Sometimes you will have to take a few steps first before your emotions agree. This can happen vice versa. However it happens for you, make sure you're going in a forward direction. I've seen many people whose lives are controlled by fear. The idea of what people may say about them terrorizes a person who lives in fear. Instead of getting excited about possibilities, they can only focus on possible disappointments. Dreaming about what could be in the future is a thought that fearful people refuse to consider, as they only focus on how bad things might get. This is not how your life should be structured. From time to time, you will need things to shake you up and cause you to be nervous so that you can have the full experience of life. Getting through something or getting over a hurdle is more enjoyable when you had to defeat external and internal opposition. The fact that you could possibly fail should give you a reason to try harder and not try less. Always be contrary to fear. When fear says no, you say yes. When fear says, "Why try?" you say, "Why not?" Refuse to be indoctrinated by fear. Fearful people will say, "I can't," and never try. If you feel you can't do something, try it anyway. By trying anyway, you'll find out where you are and how far you need to go. Not trying is dying an early death. Becoming better than you've ever been can start by just making an attempt. When you get a small taste of fighting your own fears, you'll want more of it. It feels and tastes good to step out of your own invisible box.

There are no challenges greater than the ones we present ourselves with. Outward distractions only become effective when they make their way to be inward distractions. This is true for any outward challenge. If distractions, fears, and doubts stay as outward challenges, your battle is half won. It's when the outward challenges slither their way into your thoughts that they present any real opposition. It is vital that you surround yourself with people, places, and things that are not presenting themselves as outward challenges that could possibly become inward battles. Your own creativity will sometimes work against you by imagining how things may not work out. It's better that you position yourself away from additional negativity. Don't waste your time in using your strength to fight unnecessary battles. By just not being in the midst of certain atmospheres, you can save time and energy. Fight only the necessary battles.

DEFEAT NEGATIVE EMOTIONS

Emotions are constantly given two names, which are good emotions and bad emotions. I've learned that emotions will be whatever you want them to be based on the direction you lead them in. If you focus enough on negativity, you'll utilize your emotions to fuel bad thoughts. If you focus enough on positivity, you'll then use your emotions to feel good about those thoughts. Whatever thoughts you allow your emotions to embrace, those thoughts get an extra boost of energy. No one will ever control their emotions 100 percent of the time. The good news is you can decrease the level of emotions you give to a negative thought by giving direction to your emotional fuel. You can defeat what most call a negative emotion by not giving it a negative thought. If you give any thought enough emotion, you increase your chances of bringing that thought to reality. Negative thought plus emotions equals what is called negative emotions. Emotions can be an excellent assistant to you if used correctly. Emotions can assist you when you feel low or assist you when you feel unenthusiastic. By consistently focusing on what you set out to achieve during tough times, you can command your emotions to agree with your goals. Negative emotions are defeated not by killing your emotions altogether, but by connecting your emotions with successful thinking. Just as good decisions are sometimes made by the influence of good information, so are good emotions influenced by good thoughts.

Empower yourself by not being overpowered with emotions. No one is able to make decisions for you nor influence your emotions like you can. You can get good advice, and it will always comes down to you making a decision for yourself. Decide for yourself to resist the urge to go with the flow of your emotions. Emotions, by themselves, are loose cannons because they possess no direction of their own except what you give them. Give your emotions direction, and you will be introduced to a more disciplined you. You don't have to join the army to gain discipline; just start taking responsibilities for yourself, including decisions you made based on sheer emotion.

CONTROLLING YOUR EMOTIONS IS THE REAL BATTLE

There are many people with great talents who are hindered because they may feel that they're unworthy. They are aware of their gifts, but refuse to be more than what they are. This is the result of misguided emotions. There's nothing honorable about being in a position to be more and settle for less.

You could be in a position to change your life but feel overwhelmed. Conquering your emotions and your feelings puts you in a position to do what you actually can do. Remember, conquering your emotions doesn't mean killing your emotions. Emotions are an important part of life and your emotions are an even more important part of your life. Emotions are what make us human. If your emotions control you, then they will make you an unstable human. Emotions can cause a person who believes that they can accomplish something to do whatever it takes to make their belief a reality, even if they don't have the experience or skill. On the contrary, someone could have the experience, skills, and resources, and their emotions can stop them in their tracks. You can literally command your emotions to agree with your desires. Intellect can provide a logical system to get things done. Emotions can provide a persevering attitude to see it through. When you believe in something, your emotions fuel that belief.

Lead and direct your emotions to agree with your good decisions. Good decisions should always be supported. Why not start with the support of your own emotions? If you do not give your emotions their assignment, then they will find an assignment of their own in your life. Emotions can be a helping hand if used appropriately. Just as a gun could be recreational equipment at a gun range and a weapon of destruction in war, so are the uses of your emotions in different areas of your life. When you are tempted to make wrong, irrational, and violent decisions, then use your rationality to give your emotions a new direction. When faced with the opportunity to make a very good decision, assign your emotions to back you up. Your emotions will provide the extra kick to get past what may be intimidating to you.

The spark to improve your life comes from your emotions. The "never-say-never" attitude is fueled by your emotions. Your emotions are the unseen blood, bones, and muscles of your body. Conquering your emotions thus increases the capabilities of your natural blood, bones, and muscles. When your emotions are involved in your successes, then failing is no longer an option. You'll begin to eliminate mediocre goals and dreams. The desire to rise to your peak potential becomes more of a reality than just your imagination. A driven person doesn't even have to deal with procrastination or slothfulness. When your emotions are assigned to your growth potential, they will eliminate your learning curve. Emotions have their place in all our lives; but we must decide where to place our emotions.

> *If you do not give your emotions their assignment, then they will find an assignment of their own in your life.*

It is easier to allow your emotions to drift wherever they desire than to consciously focus your emotions on specific things. The results of drifting emotions can be devastating. We've all experienced our emotions compelling us to do things that we later on regretted. So it would be your best option to consciously assign your emotions to good decisions. When you know you're making the right decision for the right reasons, you may not always get immediate support, so it is vital that you support your decisions with all you can.

THE ART OF MOVING QUICKLY

The longer you take to make a good decision, the more time you give your emotions and thoughts to side with other thoughts. Moving quickly makes you a moving target for your opposition. When you move quickly, naysayers can't ever find a time to talk to you. The dark cloud of fear cannot rest over your head, and you won't be in your own way. Being decisive gives you an edge to not miss opportunities or move slower than you have to. After you give something enough thought, move swiftly with an end result in mind. As you take your journey, remain flexible and confident that you'll gain the results you want. Uncertainty and hesitancy will slow you down and eventually stop you without warning. Of course, moving quickly is never to be done without proper analysis. After the analysis has been done, don't become over-analytical or disguise being over- analytical as preparation. Perfection will come as you move forward. Overanalyzing a decision that you are ready to make creates more imperfections and wastes valuable time. You'll have lots of goals to achieve, so it's important that you are not hindered by one decision. How soon or how late you achieve what you set out to do will depend on how fast you do or don't move quickly.

OPEN THE DOOR ANY WAY YOU CAN

Have you ever locked your keys in a car right before you had to go somewhere important? It didn't matter how you got to your keys as long as you got the door open. Sadly enough, I've been in this predicament more than once. There was such a great urgency that I was even willing to shatter the window to get to the keys. Thankfully, there were always the right people around to help me get my door open. Truthfully if there was no one around, I would've gotten the door open any way possible. Sometimes in life, there may be closed doors standing in your way. Your only job is to get the door open. I am not advocating breaking into someone's home. I am saying that kicking down doors will become necessary if you plan to succeed. Whatever the door or barrier may be, it is there for you to move it. Some doors will be closed for you and will have to be barged through. Never be discouraged because a door is shut in your face. Remember the famous saying: "Where there is a will, there's a way." If you want something bad enough, a closed door should not turn you away. From the outside looking in, overcoming something can seem so simple. I have learned that at times you must possess grit to jump over life's hurdles. Clinching your teeth, digging your soles into the ground, and pressing toward the mark is all the edge you need at times. Driving yourself fearlessly and not accepting defeat can do more than your talent will ever do. Possessing the heart of a fighter means more than being in a boxing ring. Taking a blow, staying on your feet, and not throwing in the towel display a character that few have but must possess.

Endurance is not for the faint at heart. Those who can take some pain and pressure will always rise to lead the crowd. Cowards will always eventually show their true colors. You, on the other hand, can feel the tug of fear and not give in. Barriers that stand in your way await your response. Will you do whatever it takes to get past a closed door? Or does it only take the sound of a door shutting in your face for you to fearfully shut down? Some doors must be kicked down if you expect them no longer to be in your way. To make myself clear, there may not be any actual physical kicking or violent activity. You will have to be psychologically conditioned to refuse being denied. For every no that you hear, there are some that can be turned into a yes through your persistence.

Subtleness can get you by, but only so far. This doesn't mean you should be a pompous, hard-to-deal-with, impolite imbecile. There is a difference between being outgoing and being a narcissist. When you push yourself forward, don't push yourself out of character. In desperation, it is easy to make some of the worst decisions of your life. There is no goal worth taking unethical steps to get there. Out of a burning desire to accomplish the bigger picture you have in mind, use your determinations to fight the urge to give up.

Hope is the place where your desires and dreams begin. All of your dreams and desires will come to fruition when you take action. Before they come to fruition, don't get stuck in the "hope" phase of your life. By deferring your hope, you will defer your life.

When things don't work out, reevaluate your methods, but never quit. Don't let a dream die because it may appear that you're at the end of the road.

Every part of your life may not be as pretty as you like it to be. But who has a perfect life? The road you take to change your life may be a bumpy road because most roads are. Learn to enjoy the ride and don't be discouraged so quickly by bumps on the road. If the journey started off smoothly, a bump on the road is just to let you know you're not where you used to be. Challenges are always indicators of your arrival.

Chapter 15:
Help Is Overrated

YOU! YES, YOU. YOU BUILD, conquer, achieve, and climb higher and higher, and the right help will come. It is widely preferred to occur in vice versa, to get all the help they can, then work. You must show first that you are a progressive person, because people are attracted to progress. Help is necessary, only if there's something to help. When a person would rather have their responsibility become someone else's work is when help can be overrated. Help is only necessary when you give someone the opportunity to utilize their talents in your organization. Simply passing the buck is no need for help, it is a need to take responsibility for your obligation. If the help comes first, then what will they do? Dig deep within yourself to find the initial help that you need. I promise you that enough creativity, lessons, understanding, and wisdom are inside of you that you can use for any initiative.

Before you depend on someone else to organize your life, you start the journey. Before you think it's someone else's responsibility to change, you change first. Help is necessary, but it will not be the defining factor of your success. People will help you, but you must finish the job. People will support you, but they need something to support.

Help Will Come

People are attracted to good things. So, simply become a good thing that people are attracted to. When you have something worth supporting and striving for, help is not hard to find. Never get caught in the trap of waiting for the right help to come first, because what will come your way is a reflection of what you've done so far. Waiting for the right people first will leave you at a disadvantage and dependent. You don't have to know everything, you must be willing to jump-start your goals without external support. Help will always come to those who have worthy goals. If what you seek to accomplish only edifies you, then the help may not come. Be sure that you're working toward something that will benefit others. People are drawn to selflessness. When you are selfless, you will always get a greater result. Selfless people desire the best for others and with that intention will provide the best for others. It is inevitable that great works will connect to great people. Never underestimate the power of being a force for good. All forces of good are always backed by other forces of good. If you will develop as the right person, you will in no time get the right people. I have heard many times that good help is hard to find, only to find out that is not the whole truth. Good help is hard to find for selfish people. Find ways to deliver to the world what you would want if you were on the other end.

> *Never get caught in the trap of waiting for the right help to come first, because what will come your way is a reflection of what you've done so far.*

BELIEVE IN SOMETHING GREATER THAN YOU

Believing you will have the car you want, the house you want, and the popularity you want are small goals. To be honest with you, who cares if you become rich if your wealth doesn't enrich someone else? The problem with most people is that their goals, dreams, and desires are all surrounding them and only them. Anyone seeking to obtain any level of success must realize that it will be the result of doing something good for other people. If you want to expedite your growth rate, think of others and the help they need, not what you want for you and yours. You and yours will be just fine if you and yours can give significantly to others. There is always prosperity in fulfilling a need for the needy. To some, this may be is a nonsense philosophy. And to those people, I would ask them to look at their lives and realize that their philosophy doesn't work. Losers have a tendency to adapt to losing. Winners, even when they're losing, just want to know how to win. Believing in something greater than yourself is how you win in every facet of life. Sports, businesses, relationships, marriages, and partnerships have all proven that selfishness never wins. It takes a true passion to think beyond yourself. Many call what they believe to have as great passion, but really it is selfish desire. Selfish desires exploit and abuse others for selfish gain. Great passion will deliver to people what they need.

SOME PEOPLE ARE SEASONAL

Every relationship that you have is meant to last for a specific time. It can be very frustrating when you attempt to force the relationship to live outside of its limits. Keeping people around who have outlived their purposes in your life can be agonizing for you and them. I've met many people who've made an impact on my life, and that experience with them was it. There was no more to the relationship than the month or two that we dealt with each other. If you can grasp the idea that some of your relationships are just to get you to the next place in your life, you will never be angry again for the finish of a relationship.

There are some relationships that will last much longer than others. There are some relationships that will even last until the day you die. It is important that you recognize which relationships are perpetual, seasonal, and just for right now. This is not for you to look at every person with the thought of them possibly turning his back on you. This is for you to progress without giving an ended relationship too much of your attention.

Each time you connect with someone, your life has a possibility of going in the direction that they are going. Be swift to notice if you and another individual only share a small portion of similarities. That particular portion is where you meet up. If your life and the other person's life only connect in a small way, it is a possibility that the relationship is temporal. It doesn't mean you will hate each other, it does mean you may not connect at all levels. The more you and a person connect on different levels, the longer and more in-depth the relationship will be. This is true for a partner, potential spouse, or relationships in general. Remember, you'll experience lots of people in your life. Don't be crippled by a few relationships in your life that may end abruptly and without warning. Each relationship will help you to become more well-rounded and aware of cultural differences. The more people you meet, the better of a person you become. Continually connect with new people that are full of ideas, life, and are outgoing. You will meet people who will forever change your life and vice versa. Whatever lessons you learned from previous relationships, take those lessons into every new relationship without blaming anyone for someone else's wrongdoings.

As you develop and grow, so will the type of relationships you have. This can sometimes mean the end of old relationships that you have outgrown. Outgrowing a relationship is not a reason to be upset, it's just an indicator that you have grown. Fitting back into something that you have outgrown is only good when you have lost weight to fit into old clothes. Fitting back into old relationships that are beneath your level of character and integrity is a recipe for self-sabotage. Your decisions must be centered on growth and not emotions. Too many emotional decisions will result in a life of constant up-and-down spirals. When a relationship begins to hold you back, then it's time to let it go. If you are held back, then so is everything that is connected to you. Letting go of bloodsucking relationships gives your entire life a chance.

Relationships play a bigger role in your life than some realize. If you look at your life right now, where you are has something to do with the relationships you are involved in. I lived in different states because of the people I was connected to. I love certain foods because of many relationships. I've even been in altercations that had nothing to do with me, it was my associations that involved me. If it had not been for certain relationships, there would be foods I never would've eaten, places I never would've been, and views that I never would have had. Relationships can affect you in good or bad ways. You must realize that when it's time to let a relationship go, let it go. There's too much of life that you haven't experienced yet to be stuck to one relationship. Don't be afraid to experience more. A disappointment or setback that came from a relationship cannot be the reason you don't meet new people. For any hopeful person, disappointments are just a part of life. That is why you must stay hopeful. The death of any relationship is the opportunity to birth many more relationships. The best way to live a forward-moving life is to stay connected with forward-moving people. Some people that are forward-movers can only go so far with you if they start going in another direction. If you're both going in the same direction, then it makes maintaining the relationship easier. If you're going in opposite directions, then there's no reason to delay your dreams to follow someone else.

There will be moments in your life where suddenly you're not connected to a lot of people. Those moments are to be used for studying and reevaluating your philosophies and action plans to gain the strength to press forward. Depression, anger, and grieving should not be embraced during moments of alone time. This is not to say anger, grieving, and depression won't show up. This is to say just don't embrace them. Let your downtimes only be momentary, not for a lifetime. The majority of your life should consist of your best days, not your worst. If you are coming out of your worst days, then expect your latter days to be greater and less of the same things you've experienced. What should only last for a moment, let it be for only a moment. Your time is extremely valuable and cannot be wasted on wishing for the resurrection of a dead relationship. The right partner, the right spouse, and the right people are closer to you than you think. Treat everyone with love and respect, earn the trust of other people and allow people to earn your trust. Human interaction is not to be avoided. It is to be embraced, anticipated, and improved upon. Loving life also means loving people.

YOU MAKE THE DIFFERENCE, NOT AN INSTITUTION

What makes a great business or organization is great people. There is not one institution on this planet that has a great name or great brand within itself. It is and always will be great people who've made great institutions, great countries, and great governments. So never believe that a college or employer will in itself make you great. You can go to the best school in the country and end up poor and begging. The reason for this is that the school name will not make a difference, but the person will make a difference by using what was learned while attending school. More importantly, you would have to show why you as a person, not as a college graduate, would be an asset and not liability. Don't believe the myth that as long as you have the perfect résumé, your success is guaranteed. Millions of people have built a résumé to look like a piece of art. The résumé only acts as something that shows where you've been and what you've done, not what you can do in the future and what you deserve. Displaying what you can do in the future and what you deserve can only be shown through your personality. Success is not guaranteed if you rely on the reputation of an organization and not your own people skills. Whenever I meet a child and ask them their educational goals, they always seem to believe that if they go to college, their lives would be great and without struggles. What they fail to realize is that a school is there to assist them in what they already decided for their lives. A university nor a job will give you purpose.

I am an advocate for higher education. Even though, education by itself just means you're smart. If you were on an island by yourself, just having intelligence cannot do too much for anyone. Intelligence coupled with the right philosophy and a sense of purpose will put you ahead of the typical "all I need is a degree" person. You should learn something new every day and continue to do so until you die.

ARE YOU SUPPORTABLE?

Double-minded people are generally unstable people. When your mind is made up, don't be easily swayed. Your ability to stay focused with laser-sharp precision will determine if people will supportively follow you. It is very difficult to follow the lead of someone who changes every five minutes. Wives, employees, and supporters all share the same problem when their leader is wayward. People must know that you will do what you said you'd do; otherwise, your words will be taken lightly. So ask yourself this question: "Am I supportable?" To be supported means people will hold you up, if you are an unstable surface, then you risk losing supporters. I didn't ask if you were perfect, I asked if you were supportable. I watched leaders who had great support fall because of their own wayward decisions. Are you worth supporting? Well, if you are, you must display that through consistency. People will believe you after you've been consistent in your actions and your beliefs. Don't think because you tell people to trust you that they actually will. Trustworthy people gain trust. Friendly people get friends. Supportable people get support. It's that simple.

GIVE TO GET

Respect gets you respect. Friendliness gets you friends. Whatever you seek to achieve, become attracted to it.

Who you are is what you attract. It's almost proverbial to hear of a woman going from one relationship to the next only to find the same type of person in another person. And to many, this is a Sally-sob-story. All of it could've changed if the woman changed herself. The problem was not the man that she attracted. It is the kind of person she is that attracted a certain type of man. If she continues being

> *Never expect what you're not willing to change for.*

the same person, pursuing the same interests, going to the same places, and doing the same things, well, she can expect the same people. There are over seven billion people on this earth. What are the odds that one person attracts the same type of people unless that person consistently goes to, speaks to, and connects with one type of person? Even if that type of person comes in many shapes and forms, the fact still remains that it's the same mentality and personality. The type of people we are is not defined by our hair color, shape, skin color, or ethnicity. The type of people we are is defined by our mentalities and philosophies. Similar philosophies and mentalities will always attract, despite color or cultural differences. It is important for you to become the type of person you want around you. It is redundant for a liar to expect herself to be around honest people. The same goes for a womanizer who adores his manipulative ways, expecting to find the woman of his dreams. If you stay the same, there are some things that you cannot expect to get. How could you ever achieve what you believe is stored up for a select few, excluding yourself? Instead of sitting and waiting for what you want, become the person that attracts what you want. Go ahead. Take your pick on what career you desire or what type of relationship you desire. It's all a matter of being what your goals are attracted to. If your desire is to have wealth, you must be less of a consumer. If you desire a peaceable life, then you have to eliminate calamity and confusion from your atmospheres. Never expect what you're not willing to change for. All your hopes and dreams are deferred the second you decide not to change. If you are a quitter, then you can never expect to accomplish goals that require a person that never gives up.

NEVER STOP PROVIDING

The more I give, the more I have to give. You can never give enough to a good thing or a great cause. I'm talking about more than philanthropy or charity. To every good thing, give your best. You can never sell enough of a good service. You can never say enough of the right thing. The world lacks good intentions without hidden agendas. Begin to think on the scale of what does society really need that you have or will have. You have the opportunity to bring to the world what you see that is missing. In business, politics, and philanthropy, you can provide something of quality and uniqueness. Don't count yourself out if you are not there yet. Just remember, you'll get there quicker than what you realize. Drive yourself to think like a provider. Whatever need you decide to meet, be sure it is met well.

Never stop giving your all to great ideas. The distracted and the weak wait for their time to come or be made for them. You can make your own time come by meeting a need. Providing something of substantial value is one of the secrets to life. No gimmicks, no games, no fluff—just provide something great. When you find what you can give, give it all. There are billions of people that you haven't encountered yet that would possibly need what you can give. You pick the demographic. You can pick the income bracket. Just decide to provide. Take the time to discover the masses that you can help.

Opportunity stands in front of you every day. As long as you steer, it will only steer back. Opportunity waits for no one, but is available to everyone to obtain. The best strategy for obtaining the best opportunities is to seek to become a provider and a giver. People who only look for opportunities rarely find them. To those who seek to give by providing for others, opportunities are everywhere. "How can I make people's lives better?" This should be what you ask yourself daily. Answering this question every day opens the world up to you. Those who seek to only take from others give themselves a short life span. Takers ruin relationships and whatever else they are associated with. Givers increase their value and the value of people and things that are connected to them. You have much to give and much to provide. Seeking provision only for yourself is a waste of thought and action. The best lives affect other lives in a profound way. You can actually do more for yourself by doing more for others.

Never Put Your Responsibility on Someone Else

You should expect to take full accountability for the dreams that you have. As you stay on the path to accomplish your goals, you will meet the right people. You will find the right support, and you will most likely achieve far beyond what you expected. To get there, it takes a mature mind that understands that 100 percent accountability is necessary if you intend to do great things. When you delegate tasks, you never really delegate 100 percent of the responsibility. The downside of great achievement is great risk. Take pleasure in the risk that you take because the right risk will mean the right reward. Whatever you set out to do, remember that no one can do it quite like you. Our world needs what you have. Our leadership needs your guidance, and the generations to come need your influence. Don't hold back anything from this life. This life is the only one you get. So, I encourage you to go for broke and please don't die rich. What I mean is rich in ideas and influence. By the time you die, you should have emptied out everything that was to be contributed to society. Be bold enough to question the status quo. Be brave enough to say what is different. Never accept what somebody tells you; everything has room for improvement. Everything and everyone could develop a little more. I am asking you to dedicate your life to goals, ideas, and purposes that matter. You can render no greater service to all of humanity than to make your worthy dreams come true. Believe it or not, there are a lot of people waiting for what you have to offer. You are not dropped in this life, at this time, for no reason. There is a greater reason for you being here than just going through the motions of bad jobs, bad relationships, and hoping to die one day. Every bone, every muscle you have, your brain, every cell, and every organ in your body was designed for you to live out your destiny. I hope that you come to the place where you can't wait to help others improve their lives. Don't spend another day on hoping that somebody will do what you know should be done. Fear nothing and embrace everything with positivity. No one could ever tell you how great you are to become. You and only you can find that out. Give every day that you have everything that you've got for that day. Become ready to live in the best days of your life and in the fulfillment of your dreams. Tolerate nothing and embrace the good that life has to offer you. Your opportunities are everywhere.

CONCLUSION

Your life is on its way to improving at an immeasurable rate. The right philosophy is all you need to accomplish anything you want to. Nothing or no one can hold you back. There is nothing in your way, just the best days of your life to fill up. See all that you can do in your life, leaving nothing in reserve. Experience all that you can with no regrets. Live your life with a passion that comes from within, and with the purpose that considers the well-being of other people's lives. Who knows how far you can go if you just start the journey. I believe that your greatest moments have yet to be experienced. There are people and places that you will have life-changing encounters with that you can't even imagine. Tolerate only what is necessary, and live your life to the fullest. Keep your tolerance level low for things that pull you backward. Your time is precious and should be defended from those who will trample over it. Ignore all the distractions that will attempt to steal your focus. Every call, every e-mail, and every text is not worth 100 percent of your attention. Be mindful of the things that you spend your time on, because that time will never be replaced.

Your new life awaits you with open arms, hoping that you come soon. There are many people that need to experience what difference you're going to make. Through your consistency and diligence, will people believe that you are worth who you say you are. Be brave enough to walk away from everything you don't want, to gain everything you do want. It is your choice to be as different as you're supposed to be. You are naturally authentic, and that's what will inspire others. Imitators and pretenders never inspire others, they're just inspired by someone else.

Walk toward your greatest life ever. Spend your time reaching as far as you can while stretching yourself to become the best version of you.

You are just what this world needs. Make the best contribution you could ever make by pursuing your purpose relentlessly.

Remember to live and not tolerate, that everything is not worth it, to make people believe you, to walk away, and to do it all because you can.

STAY CONNECTED

From thoughtful articles to powerful blogs and more,
MichaelFulmore.com is full of what you need for daily living.

---

www.MichaelFulmore.com

SCAN and GO straight to MichaelFulmore.com

Connect with Michael on your favorite sites

33459587R00081

Printed in Great Britain
by Amazon